Special Praise for *Making I*

"*Making Peace with Your Plate* is a refreshing and meaningful book to help you or a loved one recover from an eating disorder. What makes this book stand out is its unique format of alternating chapters. There is a 'story chapter,' which chronicles Robyn Cruze's recovery, followed by a 'therapist chapter,' which offers practical tools from seasoned eating-disorder therapist, Espra Andrus. Together this unique approach creates a powerful synergy."

—Evelyn Tribole, MS, RD
Coauthor of *Intuitive Eating*

"This revised edition of *Making Peace with Your Plate* is a beautifully written book and an exceptional resource for clinicians and our clients. Robyn and Espra take us through the journey of recovery with compassion and insight. The combined talent and expertise of these two professionals provide a wonderful view of the path one might need to take in order to recover. I have been reading books about recovery for thirty-six years, and this one is a true gem."

—**Beth Mayer**, LICSW, private practice, former executive director of
Multi-Service Eating Disorders Association (MEDA)

"*Making Peace with Your Plate* is real, honest, and full of hope. Join Robyn and Espra on a unique journey to authentic freedom. *Your* recovery awaits!"

—Jenni Schaefer
Author of *Almost Anorexic, Life without Ed*, and *Goodbye Ed, Hello Me*

"I love how clearly this book explains recovery. When I was in treatment, I always asked 'What *is* recovery?' and nobody could answer that in the eating disorder world. This book will help you define recovery and give you tools for change."

—**Ashley Hamilton**

"*Making Peace with Your Plate* provides a unique and meaningful vantage point. You will feel understood as you read Robyn's account of her struggle with an eating disorder, and you will find practical tools in the chapters authored by Espra, an experienced eating disorder therapist."

—**Jennifer L. Taitz, PsyD**
Author of *End Emotional Eating: Using Dialectical Behavior Therapy Skills to Cope with Difficult Emotions and Develop a Healthy Relationship to Food*

MAKING PEACE
WITH YOUR PLATE

MAKING PEACE
WITH YOUR PLATE

EATING DISORDER RECOVERY

SECOND EDITION

ROBYN CRUZE
and
ESPRA ANDRUS

CENTRAL RECOVERY PRESS

Las Vegas

Central Recovery Press (CRP) is committed to publishing exceptional materials addressing addiction treatment, recovery, and behavioral healthcare topics, including original and quality books, audio/visual communications, and web-based new media. Through a diverse selection of titles, we seek to contribute a broad range of unique resources for professionals, recovering individuals and their families, and the general public.

For more information, visit www.centralrecoverypress.com.

Publisher: Central Recovery Press
           3321 N. Buffalo Drive
           Las Vegas, NV 89129

24 23 22 21 20   1 2 3 4 5

Library of Congress Cataloging-in-Publication Data

Names: Cruze, Robyn, author. | Andrus, Espra, author.
Title: Making peace with your plate : eating disorder recovery / Robyn
   Cruze and Espra Andrus.
Description: Second edition. | Las Vegas : Central Recovery Press, 2019. |
   Includes bibliographical references.
Identifiers: LCCN 2019043582 (print) | LCCN 2019043583 (ebook) | ISBN
   9781949481266 (paperback) | ISBN 9781949481273 (ebook)
Subjects: LCSH: Eating disorders. | Eating disorders--Treatment.
Classification: LCC RC552.E18 C78 2019 (print) | LCC RC552.E18 (ebook) |
   DDC 616.85/26--dc23
LC record available at https://lccn.loc.gov/2019043582
LC ebook record available at https://lccn.loc.gov/2019043583

Photo of Robyn Cruze by Jessica Cruze.
Photo of Espra Andrus courtesy of Life Launch Centers.

Publisher's Note: This book contains general information about addiction and other self-destructive behaviors, and developing wellness and emotional health. The information is not medical advice, and should not be treated as such. Central Recovery Press makes no representations or warranties in relation to any medical information in this book; this book is not an alternative to medical advice from your doctor or other professional healthcare provider.

If you have any specific questions about any medical matter you should consult your doctor or other professional healthcare provider. If you think you or someone close to you may be suffering from any medical or mental health condition, you should seek immediate medical attention. You should never delay seeking medical advice, disregard medical advice, or discontinue medical treatment because of information in this or any book.

Our books represent the experiences and opinions of their authors only. Every effort has been made to ensure that events, institutions, and statistics presented in our books as facts are accurate and up-to-date. To protect their privacy, some of the names of people, places, and institutions have been changed.

Cover design by Prickly Pear Marketing and interior by Deb Tremper, Six Penny Graphics.

Love to our devoted families and fierce friends, who urge, support, drag us—and sometimes outright demand for us to have the courage to follow our dreams and share our truth.

We lovingly commit this work to all individuals everywhere who suffer with eating disorders and to all those who have been tricked into believing the lie that their worth is defined by the size and shape of their body or by any number whatsoever.

Table of Contents

Preface to the Second Edition

By Robyn Cruze

Within my past sixteen years of recovery and active mental wellness advocacy work, and since writing the first edition of this book, I have learned that I was not alone in the battle of the mind that had me vacillating between wanting to be free from my disorder and believing that I needed it to survive. While in the throes of the illness, I did not realize others felt as I did. At least 30 million individuals of all ages within the United States have a lifetime prevalence of an eating disorder.[1] Many of these 30 million, like me, struggled in silence, isolation, and desperation. Therefore, it is no surprise that many of us believe we have no choice but to listen the voice of the eating disorder. We do have a choice. We do play a role. We can recover.

Since the first edition of this book was published, I have been so humbled by the countless conversations I have had with those who struggle. I have learned that many of us fear recovery because of the underlying anxiety, depression, and other mood disorders we suffer. There is freedom in gaining the clarity that there is more to our disorder than a relationship with food, body, and control. Addressing the underlying issues that may have contributed to our drive and need for the disorder is essential.

It can feel more difficult to recover from something for which you have a primal need. We cannot just walk away from food never to eat it again. We must build a relationship with food, and with our bodies, if we want to find peace. Building a relationship takes time and commitment. We can't just leave when we get challenged. Instead we get to stay and show up for ourselves.

Use this book in conjunction with your therapist. Find a support group, a team, recovery friends, and if possible, lean on your family. Most of all

---

1 National Comorbidity Survey Replication (Hudson, Hiripi, Pope, & Kessler, 2007).

though, find your power in defining your recovery from your truth—not from the illness.

In this book, I have bared my soul. As you read my story, know that comparing and isolating are part of the effects of an eating disorder—an attempt to pick out the differences in my life circumstances, behaviors, appearance, even my upbringing, and compare them to yours to keep you in isolation by convincing you that there is no relationship between us. But there is. We know each other well. No matter what eating disorder behavior you are attempting to overcome, we can identify with the paralyzing emotional burden of the illness that has dictated our every waking hour.

Use my story and think, *If Robyn can do this, so can I.* That's my reason for writing this in the first place. That's all I want from it. Espra will give you the tools I used to help me through the recovery process. Although Espra was not my therapist, she is a match for the eating disorder. She is a compassionate one. She honors those struggling with eating disorder behavior fully. And you and I can support each other in our differences and our many similarities as we continue to gain back our power and make peace with ourselves, our world, our bodies, and indeed, our plates.

Acknowledgments

We are so grateful for all the support and help of so many who made this book a reality. A special thanks goes to our families—we love you more than you can know and desperately plead that our next and future generations among you see yourselves and others as people, not objects.

To the finest support team ever, David Nelson, Valerie Killeen, Michael Berrett, Melanee Cherry, and Hayley Giles; we are truly grateful for your expertise and your shared passion and encouragement in getting this book into the hands of those who need it most. It would have been impossible without the hours of consultation, review, and assistance you contributed. Thanks to the countless other professionals who have contributed their ideas and wisdom.

Robyn would like to give additional thanks: Lilly, Chloe, and Tim! Oh my, without you this world would not be so magical. Tim, you teach me so much about recovery and myself every day. Thank you for not ever allowing us to play it safe in a world so full of bigness. To the rest of my loving family for allowing me to bring you on this journey of sharing my story as I see it, and in turn yours. To my tribe of women who use their voice and gifts to make a difference daily and who hold me accountable to do the same: Andi O'Reilly Sullivan, Rebecca Berg, Emily Eby, Dana Mestek, Jenni Schaefer, Stephanie Chao-Parkes, Nicole Owenga-Scott and all you other strong, powerful women I am so blessed to have surrounding me. I am indebted to all of you for your friendship, love, and personal wisdom—there are indeed, so many of you. I love you dearly.

Espra would like to give additional thanks: To Jenn for showing me the world in color, reminding me to laugh, believing in me—and for cheerleading, consoling me, and suffering alongside me for this cause. To Mom and Pop for assuring me that I can do anything I decide to do. I am blessed to have you all and your daily reminders that I am loved. To my family and friends for urging me that my voice can make a difference, enduring my diatribes about dieting and body lies, and being the huge part of my fountain of blessings that you are. To Brenda (for your sacrifices to make this work a reality), the founders of Center for Change (for believing in me and being my mentors), my DBT consultation team and friends (for keeping me from losing my way), and the many clients, families, and colleagues who have trusted me and passed on their wisdom and knowledge. Thank you Kristie Lemmon for dragging me into, um, I mean, inspiring and supporting my journey to heal shame in myself and others. To my Life Launch Centers partners for sharing my passion for life resilience and working to spread it. We've got this.

And to Francyne Cruze, who epitomized all mothers around the world who walk the path with their children in a desperate search in understanding and ending eating disorders. God bless you.

Introduction

Robyn

Having an eating disorder felt much like treading in deep water with only my nostrils above the waterline. I was drowning along with my dreams and purpose. The food, the diets, the purging, and the harsh voice I labeled the eating disorder with that kept me in my place—all of it filled my mind endlessly. Toward the end of the disorder, there was room for nothing else.

One night, I think as a kid, I heard on the news or read in a book somewhere, about some form of Japanese torture practice in which individuals being interrogated were confined in a chamber and unable to move as one drop of water at a time dripped constantly on their temple. Although I do not dare to suggest that I know what one goes through under such inhumane circumstances, over the years in the eating disorder, when I felt I could escape neither from it nor myself, I felt a deep sense of torture. Yet I also believed I needed the behavior, or rather, the control found in the eating disorder behavior to protect me from life, from others, and from myself. Eating disorders are powerful illnesses that need to be addressed far beyond our relationship with food and body.

Toward the later part of my illness, I knew it was only a matter of time before it either killed me or I took my own life. The truth is, 30 to 80 percent of those who have an eating disorder also struggle with a mood and/or anxiety disorder.[2] This must be addressed on our journey to recovery as well.

Eating disorders have the highest mortality rate of any mental illness.[3] This is true. What also is true is that you can take back all the power you gave to the

2 Ulfvebrand, S., Birgegard, A., Norring, C., Hogdahl, L., & von Hausswolff-Juhlin, Y. (2015). Psychiatric comorbidity in women and men with eating disorders: Results from a large clinical database. *Psychiatry Res*, *230*(2), 294-299.
3 Arcelus J. et al. Mortality rates in patients with anorexia nervosa and other eating disorders. *Archives of General Psychiatry*, *68*(7):724-731.

disorder—at any time. I promise you can do it. You can begin to find comfort in saying no to the voice of the eating disorder and gain a new sense of power. By the end of this book, it is my sincere hope that you will have discovered how truly powerful you are! Oh, and heads up, your power is far greater than the power you may think the eating disorder holds over you.

Today, I live a life driven by purpose and full of feeling. My life continues to feel like it has been upgraded from a black-and-white TV to a colorful, high-definition system with surround sound. Yet it did not always feel like that during the early stages of recovery. Recovering from an eating disorder is like shaking out a rug under which you have stored all your dust and dirt for years; the dust and dirt are blinding. They are gritty, and particles fly everywhere.

To realize myself in recovery fully, the recovery process needed to be adapted to my safety requirements and self-discovery along the way. This will be true for you too. I needed a recovery plan that changed along with me. I also knew this process was of no real use unless I worked with professionals specializing in eating disorder, depression and anxiety, trauma, and substance use. Even after I had been free from the eating disorder behaviors for seven years, I still needed to address my anxiety and depression and my periodic use of alcohol to self-medicate. Many of us discover that we have a propensity for substance use. We are not alone. Up to 50 percent of those who struggle with an eating disorder also will be susceptible to substance use disorder.[4] Treatment for substance use varies, as does the level in which we struggle with substance use, or the type of substance. If you think this may be you, get curious with your recovery; there are many different recovery paths. Find the one that works for you. Find power in your recovery, not punishment.

I remember one cold Colorado morning after I had given myself alcohol poisoning. Having lost my mum one month before giving birth to my first child, I lay in the fetal position, unable to get up. I lay full of remorse and hopelessness in a bout of relentless depression and anxiety. I had resorted to using alcohol rather than eating disorder behaviors to cope with my grief. I had hit yet another valley in my recovery, but it had nothing to do with eating and food. My husband, Tim, who happens to be an interventionist and

---

4 Brewerton, Timothy D., & Dennis, Amy Baker (Eds.). (2014). *Eating disorders, addictions and substance use disorders: research, clinical and treatment perspectives*. Berlin: Springer Verlag.

family recovery coach (I know! You can't make this shit up.) identified the issue immediately and checked me into substance use rehab.

During my stay, a counselor requested I get an eating disorder evaluation because I had a history of the disorder and a fierce hatred of being weighed. They wanted to be certain that any eating disorder behavior would not become an obstacle to my recovery from substance use. It was during that evaluation I met Espra. Although it was a short meeting, I left her office thinking, *here's a woman who has taught me more about eating disorders in two hours than I knew already*. Let's face it; many of us who have struggled with eating disorders have studied so much about our disorder that we believe we could have PhDs in nutrition and eating disorder psychology. After all, we are perfect researchers, perfect students, and perfect eating disorder conformists. But Espra brought with her years of knowledge and experience in eating disorder treatment, Dialectical Behavior Therapy (DBT), and a glorious sense of humor that could pierce through the most resistant character. I had recovered from the eating disorder long before, but she understood that a residue of negative self-talk had remained with me long after the eating disorder behavior had ended. Although the negative thoughts no longer dictated my actions, they still needed to be challenged and ultimately put to rest. During that meeting, Espra was able to guide me in removing the negative self-talk and shutting down any remnant of eating disorder thinking by showing me that I truly had the power to do it myself. To be clear, without Espra, this book would not be possible. I am honored and profoundly grateful for her work and her friendship. *Thank you, dear Espra.*

Since the writing of the first edition of this book, I have learned so much about the labels of "fully recovered" and "full recovery." I have seen many individuals work tirelessly in their eating disorder recovery only to get tripped up by comparing themselves to those who have claimed such titles. Please know there is no textbook or research study that will definitively tell you what "full recovery" means. But I'm not sure it matters. In fact, I worry that it becomes too much of a focus for many who are contending with this disorder and interferes with the process of recovery itself.

When I was in recovery, there were no such labels. So, a word of caution here: Do not, I repeat, *do not*, trip yourself up by imagining there is some recovery success club or police. Please don't do it to yourself. Don't find one more thing with which to compare or judge yourself. Your recovery is sacred and is unique to you, just like your body, and trying to be like others is not a far distance from the painful comparing in eating disorders that destroys lives. Comparing ourselves to others is a painful trait for most humans. You define your own recovery.

My personal definition of recovery is this: I do not binge, purge, or starve, and my body or food intake no longer dictates my daily activities. In today's society, women, men, and children of all shapes, races, and economic statuses, are susceptible to the media and their peers' judgments. However, in my recovery, regardless of the body-image-ideal-of-the-moment our culture deems worthy, that destructive ideal no longer defines me. To me, recovery means that my true self, not the words of the eating disorder, prevails, and for the love of God, I define what it means to feel beautiful and look good.

You define your own recovery.

I'll end by saying this: No one told me that to be in recovery does not mean accepting yourself from the very beginning. In fact, that is impossible. However, it is possible to "own" your story. No one told me that recovery is a combination lock that, if I have the courage to open it, will take me back to my true self and all my dreams and life purpose. Grab onto this book and the words of hope within it and breathe it in whenever you are in doubt or fear about this recovery process. You are worthy of recovery, whatever that looks like to you. If you fall, you have not failed. You simply need to get back up, brush yourself off, and be willing to take the next best step in your recovery— without shame. Toward your dreams. Toward your truth.

I'm with you!

Espra

For years, the universe nudged me toward adding the treatment of individuals suffering with eating disorders to the focus of my work as a therapist. I resisted. Then life, with the tapestry it weaves from beauty and tragedy, outright catapulted me toward eating disorder work. As a believer that we all have choices, I felt that I had two choices: 1) work with eating disorders or 2) work with eating disorders.

Two decades ago, I sat in the boardroom with the founders of one of the top eating disorder treatment programs in the nation. I admired them, both as amazing therapists and people, and they had more than eighty years of collective clinical experience among them. As I confessed my inadequacies in treating eating disorders, one of them clarified, "If you weren't a good therapist, we wouldn't be having this conversation. We'll teach you what you need to know about eating disorders." And teach me they did; their wisdom and interventions often flowed out of them as casually as if they were telling me how to water a plant. Wishing my brain were a sponge, I watched my mentors as they worked, and I scribbled down their words. They watched over me, taught me, and tirelessly passed on their knowledge, mostly to quell my episodes of panic.

I excessively worry that I will not be able to contribute the very best treatment options that are available to a client or family seeking my help with their recovery journey. This fear keeps me spending crazy amounts of time, money, and energy working to learn and deliver the latest tools that are researched to be effective for treating eating disorders and the phenomena that drive and result from them. My seeking has led me to become intensively trained in delivering therapies like Dialectical Behavioral Therapy (DBT), mindfulness training, Eye Movement Desensitization and Reprocessing (EMDR), Cognitive Behavioral Therapy (CBT), shame resilience, and interventions to help heal the brain and release it from the shackles of constant self-punishment.

These and other interventions have been found to be effective in treating Bulimia Nervosa and Binge Eating Disorder. While it has been even more complicated to identify therapeutic approaches that show effectiveness in treating Anorexia Nervosa, I find that many clients appreciate knowing how to use DBT skills to regulate emotion and tolerate distress as they take back their power from the eating disorders. Radically Open DBT skills help individuals who struggle with high levels of overcontrol, as is found in Anorexia Nervosa.

Many of the interventions I use in treating eating disorders come from traditional therapeutic modalities, while others were discovered or developed in the trenches alongside clients, families, and colleagues on the eating disorder battlefield. Many of the techniques I use I have learned from the most informed eating disorder experts of all—my clients. Some of these experts have taught me in subtle and almost imperceptible ways, and others have taught me with passionate critiques. If held with an open mind, an open heart, and a desire to be a part of healing, all of these can be useful.

Despite more than twenty years of training and practice, I don't feel like an expert in treating eating disorders. If anyone touts themself as such, you should run away from them. A true expert, who had conquered her eating disorder after eighteen years of battling it, once entered my office merely for a one-time consult as a matter of protocol for the program where she was seeking other help. We spoke of her recovery journey, one that led her to a fulfilled life that had been free of eating disorder behavior for seven years. We spoke of how lingering thoughts about her worth and value depending on her body size and shape—thoughts she knew to be untrue—niggled in the back of her mind, even though her life was not influenced at all by eating disorder behaviors or urges. I tossed only a couple of ideas, which I'd seen as beneficial to others with similar struggles, her way, and we experimented with those in my office before Robyn went on her way.

It was two years after that brief encounter when Robyn called me to see if I would be interested in writing a book with her. It turns out that writing a book was on my bucket list, and I had been impressed with Robyn's recovery work and mindset. So when she told me of her idea to write a book to help others recover from eating disorders, I thought the universe was urging me to pay attention.

Robyn wanted another voice to speak about recovery "from the other side of the therapy room," and wondered if I would consider being that voice. While this was my dream, it gave me permission to be imperfect, because Robyn's recovery story fills in any holes that my work alone might leave. I knew I needed to accept the call.

Robyn and I share a passion: getting the message that it is possible to break free and heal from eating disorder behaviors into as many hands as possible. One way to do that is to expose the illusion and lies that eating disorders have sold to more than one out of every ten people, of all ages, in the United States.

I cannot begin to count how often I have clenched my teeth and snarled, like Robyn, "#@*! you, eating disorder, you're not going to win!" I hate eating disorders! They convince amazing, intelligent, and talented people that they are worthless and unworthy of love and connection. Eating disorders convince individuals who fear they are inadequate that getting their food or body to be a certain way will make up for their imperfect selves to protect them from being banned from the love and acceptance that are the right and need of every human being.

So often I have thought, *there's got to be something,* something *that I can do better or more intensely to shake the hearts of these beautiful souls. What can I do to help them see that eating disorders thrive on half-truths, lies, illusions, and discouragement? What can I do to help others step back and see a bigger picture that exposes the devastation (to ourselves, our loved ones, our children, and our society) that eating disorders leave in their wake? What can I do to help those who suffer with eating disorders see that both recovery and a better life exist, and that recovery has rewards that reach far beyond a mere existence of using sheer willpower to hold eating disorder behaviors at bay?*

As Robyn said, there is no formal definition of the exact point called eating disorder recovery, so both partial and full recovery are still defined based on an individual's experience of eating disorder symptoms or the absence of symptoms. Not everyone escapes eating disorder behaviors and thoughts 100 percent, but chances increase dramatically for those who enter the race, begin it, and stay in it. Recovery is more attainable to those who keep trying. Decrease eating disorder behaviors, no matter how long it takes. Set goals to increase self-kindness and self-respect along the way. Neither Robyn nor I want to activate your shame and guilt and hopelessness by pretending there are only two extremes in eating disorder recovery, full and complete recovery or failure. There are unlimited places in between that truly result in a better life.

Recovery is more attainable to those who keep trying.

There are also many different models to recovery. DBT is just one of them. We have found that a combination of tools is required. Take what you want and leave the rest. In recovery your goal is to eat when you are physically hungry and stop eating when you are physically full, most of the time. You want to allow yourself to eat a wide range of foods rather than depriving yourself to a narrow range. When you eat more than your body needs, the next step is to work toward compassion rather than compensating by ingesting more calories, spending calories, or restricting them later. You work to remember that it will sort itself out. Recovery means that you might be upset when you do not like the way your body looks or the way your clothing fits, but those thoughts and feelings do not consume you or dictate how you spend your day. You engage in regular physical activity with the goal of enjoyment and life balance instead of spending calories. You are able to focus on your values, relationships, and priorities beyond the size or shape of your body, regardless of your eating or how you feel about your body.

You can be in recovery and, like most people, still dislike parts of your body, think about dieting, or sometimes use food to cope with emotions. The difference in recovery is that you are committed to recognizing the eating disorder's traps and doing whatever is necessary to steer clear of them or get out as soon as possible after falling into them. Your energy and behaviors are spent pursuing your values and goals more than making or keeping your body a certain way. You work to remember that you are not an object whose worth can be reduced to numbers. For example, if I find a wallet with a hundred dollars in it my long-term values would lead me to return it, but I am certain the thought would occur to me that I could keep it. Once I observe the gap between my long-term values and my immediate thoughts and urges, I might call a friend and ask her to remind me that following my long-term values and returning the money would leave me feeling better in the long run. I might think I am bad or dishonest for having the thought to keep the money. Being who I want to be, however, is in what I do with those thoughts and the behaviors I choose. My clients generally agree that eating disorder recovery means working to avoid eating disorder behaviors even when thoughts or urges to do otherwise are present. Individuals generally consider themselves fully recovered when the thoughts and urges to engage in eating disorder behaviors are merely a blip on the radar that uses no more energy than a fleeting irritation.

Both Robyn and I are convinced and are committed to spreading the word that there is hope in eating disorder recovery—not only hope of muddling through some miserable existence, but hope that your life can have more peace, fulfillment, and meaning in pulling out of the eating disorder's clutches. I refuse to fall for the lie that eating disorders will prevail.

Robyn and I speak a lot about "fighting" in this book. We want you to understand that illnesses, eating disorders included, are technically not treated by "fighting" them but by understanding what is needed to accept the nature of that which is affecting us and work with our body, mind, and emotions to give ourselves all we can. We must work to identify the best ways to care for the illness and help it be as stable as possible and hopefully even heal completely. For example, fighting cancer does not include being mean to oneself; it means serious self-care in very specific ways and in the face of not knowing what the outcome might be. It means "fighting" anyway.

Anger gives us energy to push through obstacles that stand in the way of our goals, and my anger, in part, has fueled this work. Both Robyn and I have channeled our anger to help us find courage to act. Courage, as any soldier fighting in a war will tell you, is not an emotion. Courage is taking action even when you are scared to death. There are tools we can use to help us in these challenges. We must be awake (we call this mindfulness) and prepared to act on opportunities to align ourselves with our values and goals. It has taken tremendous courage for Robyn and I to embark on this journey to help others find hope. We invite you to come along with us.

Your world, your life, and your dreams
are right here waiting for you.

*Today I will allow myself to try something
different in order to claim my life.*
—Robyn

1.

Enough Already

Cory Jones and Hollywood Dreams

By Robyn

It all began outside the school canteen (cafeteria) as I sat bingeing on the five bags of potato chips that I'd purchased for recess. It was the first time I'd consciously decided to forgo my usual order of a sandwich for a larger quantity of food. The act was calculated and numbing. I was eleven years old.

Cory Jones was sitting across from me, trying to impress me by eating a fly. "Dare me to eat it?" he shot off, cupping his hand over a trapped fly caught between his hand and the concrete.

"Yeah," I muttered, in between shoveling in potato chips. I was in a comforting trance that I would later realize was telling of all my binges to come. Just a day or so prior, my mum had told our family that she may be dying. Mum had an autoimmune illness—lupus. Back when I was a child, it was a rare disease and treatment was very limited. Mum was running out of treatment options and her kidneys were beginning to fail. There at the dining table, the night before Cory ate a fly, I commenced a crippling battle with an eating disorder that I would fight until the age of twenty-nine.

Just like the definition of someone who struggles with substance use disorder is different from that of a heavy drinker, there is a difference between someone suffering from an eating disorder and someone preoccupied with his or her weight because of the unrealistic expectation of our broken body-image-ideal culture.

I can be preoccupied with my food, yet understand and consider the consequences of my dieting and what it can do to my body and mind if I am not treating it correctly. If I need to make changes due to these consequences, although it's uncomfortable, I am able to make them for my well-being. However, when I am struggling with an eating disorder, I feel I must do these behaviors, no matter the cost. I can weigh the cost and the benefits, but no matter what, the benefits of eating disorder behavior appear to outweigh my need to be physically safe.

For example: My friend Sarah said to me one day, after I'd spent a Christmas holiday alone in a blackout from diet pills, "The difference between you and me, Robyn, is that I am not willing to kill myself to look good." I was. I didn't want to die, but I didn't care how close I came to death if it gave me a chance to be at the weight I believed I "should" be. This is the definition of an eating disorder in a nutshell.

The eating disorder took on many forms as I vacillated from binge eating to bulimia to deprivation. I chose what was the most powerful "f*ck it" button that would place an immediate halt to my current feelings. I chose what made me feel the most in control—even when it appeared I was out of control—I chose it. It was that feeling of power that saved me from the reality that I actually had no control in my life—over my mum's health, my parents' rocky relationship, how people felt about me, my crippling anxiety and the thoughts that went along with it, and how I felt about myself. Sometimes, I felt like I had the eating disorder behavior under control, that I could sustain the deprivation and grossly compromised living, and I found hope in it. Sometimes, I let go of all control of food, life, and myself. I was not simply "conscious of my weight," I was living life from the perspective of the eating disorder, lost beneath the rubble of the illness and extreme pain. Sometimes, I also wanted to die because I saw no way out.

For the longest time, I wished I'd never had an eating disorder. I remember a day while working in Spain when I realized that my history was, well . . . mine. A history that I would never be able to change, no matter what I did. I carried great shame about how my story looked and how my truth would sound to others—if ever spoken. That in itself kept me fighting for control over the eating disorder for more years than necessary. I didn't want to own my truth. I wanted someone else's story that looked more glamorous and successful than mine. I wanted to be like everyone in Hollywood, or at least the image I projected upon them.

I knew the manipulation that went along with modeling and the images in glamour magazines—the airbrushing that often took place after unimpressive photo shoots. I even knew this firsthand. My first career was as a professional TV and film actress. I knew the poses to strike during a photo shoot to promote a show I was on to make my jaw line look defined and pointy. I knew what angle the photographer needed to shoot to make me look rail-like after a night of bingeing. I knew that most of the "glamorous world" was smoke and mirrors, fake; but somehow, I wanted to be the exception. I was seeking perfection, which would make me worthwhile—safe from any potential ridicule. It was a state of mind that could never be obtained. The bar rose as my weight went down. It was all an illusion.

I believed that being thinner made me more lovable. Everyone said it wasn't the truth. I *knew* it was. What I saw when looking at friends was how they appeared to get more attention for being thinner and more beautiful. That's what the eating disorder told me—or rather the scary thoughts that I personalized as the eating disorder. I saw women who, on the outside, appeared to be okay in their own skin, and that was stunning to me. I had never known what that felt like. I longed to feel like I imagined they felt. I got further and further away from reality because I was stuck in this tiny world of aiming to be someone who wasn't real. I was stuck in a lie. I thought if I could just reach an ideal, then I could start living. But as I chased the ever-illusive body ideal, life was happening without me.

I inherited the perception that what you look like counts. When my family (including me) teased my dad by calling him "Fatty Patty," it seemed so funny at the time, but I also understood it to mean that "fat people" are not respected, and society reflected that daily. He appeared an easy target and willing enough to play along. He, too, would seek his comfort, but it was in a six-pack of beer.

Growing up, I learned the language of the ideal body culture. It's scary to say that not much has changed between growing up in the 80s and now. God, what I wouldn't give to tell my younger self do not, I repeat, *do not* perm your already curly hair just because everybody is doing it. More importantly, I would tell her that the body size ideal created by designers, into which only a mere few will fit and the rest of us are screwed, is a setup. It's a hoax. But that wouldn't have mattered to my younger self because eating disorders are not really about the size of our bodies.

I did want to fit in and disguise myself in the herd, and I didn't want to be like Dad—a walking target because of his beer belly and love for eating one loaf of bread in one sitting. I did want to control my outsides so that my insides would feel better. It gave me a sense of purpose and a focus that kept my eyes on the surface, above the rug, so I didn't have to look at the fear and vulnerability trapped beneath.

For many years I hid in the aphorism "tomorrow it will all be different." Life is difficult, and starting recovery is even more difficult. I know that to be true. But I also know that recovery is a place where you get to pardon yourself for not being perfect. Early recovery is like building faith in a power greater than yourself; you may catch glimpses of not feeling alone or miracles that touch you, but you cannot see this power of recovery, for it is not yet tangible, so it is a leap of faith.

There will never be a "right" time to start recovery. I just had to make a decision, followed by action and willingness to be uncomfortable. I needed to allow myself to sit with feeling out of control and uncertainty so that I had a chance to rewire my brain, learn that my feelings of discomfort wouldn't kill me, and write a new narrative for my life that wasn't the narrative of the eating disorder. I had to sit with the fear long enough to prove the fear wrong. It takes hard work and commitment and time, to be sure. But here's the thing: I was committed to trying to appease the eating disorder for many years, and that was hard, too! The years I spent in the eating disorder were not worth it and amounted to nothing. Whether I was bingeing, purging, starving, or using alcohol and other drugs to prevent myself from eating, the outcome was the same. For a short period of time, I got to numb my scary thoughts, my anxiety, my insecurities, and my shame. But over time, I got nothing, achieved nothing . . . except a story that I now get to change.

I use to think I was a "bad," "broken," "weak" person for having an eating disorder, or any other mental illness for that matter, but I now consider myself to have been a very smart little girl who did her best with the options available to her. That little girl stumbled upon behaviors that provided comfort in a world where everything felt out of control—unsafe—scary. The behaviors of the eating disorder became a security blanket for life's challenges, until they *became* life's challenges, which she then had to save herself from.

It takes a combination of human traits and circumstances for a person to be predisposed to an eating disorder. My therapist friend Jeana says that when it comes to becoming susceptible to an eating disorder, DNA loads the gun and life pulls the trigger. I totally get that. Mental illness is in my DNA.

I was loved. Adored. *Truly.* My sister, brother and I were clearly Mum and Dad's greatest gifts in their lives. Having my family's genes, alone, did not cause the eating disorder to occur. However, with my personality traits and then a traumatic event, the trigger was pulled.

I was a highly sensitive and intuitive child who began to be anxious before the eating disorder, even long before Mum was diagnosed with lupus. As I kneeled on the dirt beneath the backyard stairwell pretending to be a botanist, I delved deep into my imagination. I made sure everything was kept tidy and in its place, even the items I only imagined. I patted the dirt as if it were magical soil and planted the seeds that were, in reality, orange seeds from that morning's breakfast. Then *bam!* Out of nowhere (or at least that's how it felt,) random worries I found myself unable to control would invade my make-believe thoughts.

Then one night at the dining table, during the traumatic event of being told that my most beloved person in the entire universe might be taken from me—bang! My mind became a breeding ground for an eating disorder, rich in fertilizer and sprayed with Miracle Grow.

To combat the onset of the mental disorder, I did what any little fighter would do. I put on her superhero cape and panties (metaphorically speaking) and looked for a solution to soothe me in a world that felt unbearable. I found food. It was the fastest, most accessible medicine I could find that dulled the revving anxiety motor within. All my scary thoughts stopped when I put food in my mouth.

Gabor Maté, a physician with a background in family practice and a special interest in childhood development and trauma, and author of *In the Realm of Hungry Ghosts*, once said, the question is ". . . not why the addiction, but why the pain?" Amen. My use of food and later my unhealthy relationship with alcohol was medication for all the emotional pain I had swept under the rug. The only problem was that over time, it became more and more difficult to keep the pain hidden.

Both you and I did our best with what we had to help us survive. We found food, and the manipulation thereof. Maybe you are like me; when

I first discovered food could talk—to be a companion, it spoke to me with the same calming voice my mother did. Then it turned on me and became violent. The thing to which I turned to calm me was the very thing I began to realize was killing me.

When I commenced my recovery journey, I had to learn to fight for my life, the same way my mum fought for hers from her physical illness, lupus.

How to Follow Your Dreams and Not Your Critics

By Espra

Robyn's passionate story of her awakening and travels (wonderful and heartbreaking) along the path of her recovery is the foundation of this book. Robyn and I endeavor to create a way for you to see her path of struggle and recovery in action, as well as offer you tools to help you in your own recovery. We are both here to help you find your way, to encourage you and support you as you make your individual journey toward your own recovery.

There is power in learning and using skills to change our behaviors, urges, thoughts, and feelings, rather than relying on insight alone. So this book is not about "why." It's about using practical tools to help you pull away from the clutches of the eating disorder. It is about helping you find the willingness to do whatever it takes to put those skills toward living your life and dreams beyond the dictates of an eating disorder.

As Robyn discovered, energy spent on repeatedly asking why you have an eating disorder, and waiting for the answer before you can start recovery, is energy misspent. Instead, taking continual, small steps to help you align with your values and goals will keep you on target. Focus on questions such as, "What is the next action I need to take right now?" Persistently asking this question and finding even one small step to take in that direction is what recovery is made of.

> **Taking continual, small steps to help you align with your values and goals will keep you on target.**

If you are reading this book as someone who is struggling from an eating disorder, it is a great start. You are likely thinking in some way about recovery. Beginning to look at recovery starts with an event (external or internal) that you cannot afford to forget. For example, Robyn had a moment of awareness, a recognition of the chaos of the whole darn thing. This tumultuous life is caused by the same eating disorder behavior that promises to give you control over your life by managing your food, body size, or shape. If you step back and really look you will see yourself lying, stealing, consuming, or avoiding food at any cost to your loved ones, relationships, yourself, or your self-respect. Perhaps you see that these are the same relationships, events, and opportunities that you desperately want to love and enjoy.

Was there a catastrophe (related to your disorder) that occurred or that you barely avoided? Have loved ones told you how much your eating disorder is hurting them or that they are afraid for you? Did a significant other tell you that something has to give—the eating disorder or the relationship—or did a medical provider tell you that this really is a big deal because it is destroying your body? Regardless of the reason that brought you here, try not to judge whether your motivation is "right" or "wrong." (The eating disorder is probably already doing that for you!) The important thing is that you are here. Let's take it from this point.

We have included tools in each chapter to help you look at various parts of your eating disorder. Work with the tools in your own way, and keep them in one place as your tool kit for future use. You will need them throughout your recovery. Here is your first tool:

What made you step back and think about recovery? There is no right or wrong answer. What occurred the instant before you said, "Enough! I'm sick of this eating disorder!"? Write it down. Then write it on several sticky notes or cards. Put them on your mirror, in your wallet, in your car, or wherever you look throughout the day. Begin to bombard yourself with this reminder of "what" until it begins to physically lay down a pathway in your brain, which it will with repetition and time.

Do everything possible to remember this reason. You cannot afford to forget what made you decide to take back your life.

This tool will help you get what you need, just like Robyn who found what she needed—a way to sustain her decision. When the power of the moment passes, these reminders of the price you have paid for your eating disorder will be fuel that will help you find motivation again. A big part of recovery is finding ways to discover and fuel motivation when it sneaks out or runs away. If you don't, your eating disorder will smugly step back in without you noticing.

 It helps to get clear on the values or guiding principles for your journey through hard things as well as this life in general. There are many resources online to help you get clear about what values are important to you. Once you get some ideas about your guiding principles or values, it helps to narrow them down to two that you want to work on aligning with right now in your life. Write those down. Put them up where you can see them. This is fuel to help keep you moving forward in any of your life journeys.

We act on what we sincerely value. Be careful. We do not act very well on values we want to have (but don't) or values others want for us (but we don't).

Each second brings a new chance to choose and to act in the direction of recovery, no matter what happened the moment before. Even the moments when you trip, fall, or stop to rest must not be confused with quitting the race. Recovering from this eating disorder takes a lifelong commitment that you keep or return to one breath at a time. There is no recovery formula or solution that covers all eating disorders or all individuals. However, we believe that our guidelines, if used and committed to (again and again), will help you find and sustain or return to long-term recovery. I predict that you will box yourself in at times by telling yourself that you are different, that your eating disorder is more harsh or more powerful—or not as harmful— and that you really are worthless and unlovable. Please believe me . . . *this is not the truth!* Right now, Robyn and I need you to trust us. And we promise, with time, you will begin to be able to trust yourself.

No amount of controlling, restricting your food or calories, or binge eating will remove your fears or make you a better person.

So, enough! No amount of controlling, restricting your food or calories, or binge eating will remove your fears or make you a better person. It is draining and fleeting. There is no solid ground to be found where the eating disorder will allow you to feel as if you have arrived at the place where you are enough. The scale will not define your worth or the amount of love you receive from other people. And eating disorders cannot be, never have been, and never will be cured by attempting to control your body or by being "better" at dieting. The idea that it is even possible is a lie, and you've been cheated. It's time to start this journey, one that really can help you take back your life. Your dreams are waiting. Robyn and I promise to show you ways to take what seems impossible and help it seem possible, and also doable, in a most liberating and inspiring way.

You are well on your journey now.

Doing something despite the fear of failure is courage.

Today I will take on the very task I fear I cannot do.
With this courage, I will write a new story for myself
and my life, where anything can happen, where
anything is possible . . . especially recovery.

—Robyn

2.

Take a New Stance

Jarred Marshmallow and Maltese Hips

By Robyn

The booming, insistent thoughts of an eating disorder gradually overshadowed the soothing sounds I heard from opening five packets of potato chips that day outside Kanwal public school. Yet, even when I felt I'd had enough of the eating disorder, I was still waiting for the willingness to begin my recovery that would replace the relief I found that day outside the canteen. It took many years for me to get to a place where I was ready to take the necessary steps toward recovery. I wanted to experience a sensation so powerful it would ignite something primal within, something that could make me resistant to the voice that told me I could not succeed.

It was true that during the eighteen years of the eating disorder, I had moments of "success"—times the eating disorder celebrated, like when I reached a goal weight or, even better, below. These successes, however, were only big enough to keep me hooked to the disorder, and far apart enough to fuel my obsession further—kind of like the rabbit chasing a carrot on a stick.

In the illness, I looked at the eating disorder as if it were its own person, as if it were trying to consume me—take me over. It's not its own person, and it has no real voice, but when in it, that's how it felt. The more I used the behaviors to numb my feelings, the more it felt as if I was becoming the disorder. Slowly the dreams for my life and myself that I so adamantly believed in and took steps toward were replaced with the need to do the behavior of the eating disorder so I could keep my fears of living at bay.

So, when it came time to step into the early stages of recovery by not doing many of the behaviors, I was petrified, to say the least. Petrified of all the feelings that would rise to the surface, but mostly, petrified of how I would look if I allowed myself to honor what my body was telling me with what I have come to refer to as my "body's mind." Hell, I didn't even know my body had its own intelligence that could actually tell me what it needed to eat, if only

I listened. Even if this enlightening piece of physiological truth had penetrated my mind, I wouldn't have trusted it. I really believed I was different. *I mean, look at my gene pool*, I said to myself. *I am part Maltese. I am supposed to have large hips and round cheeks (on both ends)!* The truth is that genes will always influence our size. There is no way of changing bone structure. The insanity for me was that I was convinced that I had the ability to starve off my destiny of large hips and a lady mustache. In fact, I still had hips, even at my thinnest. (Though I had never had a trace of facial hair—that was all in my head.)

At the end of the disorder an atmosphere of urgency began to permeate me. I felt a deep need to get on with my life. I had wasted so much of my time. It created an anxiety in me that made me scramble for solutions in quick fixes. I imagined the time it would take to wade through the mess of the illness and seek recovery. This was time I didn't have the luxury of losing. It truly felt like recovery (the long way) would take truckloads of time and effort I did not have to give.

If I could just get to the ideal weight first, *then* I would be able to commit to recovery. *Seriously, how can I live with myself as I am and be okay?* I thought. Reaching my ideal weight would free me from the hourly obsession about how I looked, and the calculating and reviewing of food I ate or didn't eat. It would free me from the daydreaming about what I would achieve once I hit my perfect weight, how I would maintain my perfect weight once I got there (and I would get there this time), why it would all work out, what people would think of me then, what I would think of me then . . . *When I reach my perfect weight, I will be free and ready to move forward*. It made perfect sense to me. This became my every breathing moment's goal. But little did I know I would never, ever achieve it. It was like trying to catch a genie to grant me wishes—they aren't real, so it was never possible.

And so spiraled my life. My isolated existence brought with it darkness brushed with tiny sparks of light that were just enough to keep me from ending it all. The highs usually came when I succeeded in starving myself for some precalculated, nonsensical period of time, or while I binged as I read the next new hopeful fad-diet book. The new diet plan provided an elaborate and convincing explanation of why I couldn't lose weight any other way. I feared that if I didn't have something that provided me hope and a solution straight after a binge, such as a new diet to start over with, I would not be able to endure the pain of sitting with the shame and hatred for myself that followed. Then I would declare, "This time it will be different."

But I was always left in the same place. Nothing changed. I was convinced I was still a nobody, a failure, a reject. I would again be thrown into the dull madness of feeling lost at sea, deep in the eating disorder. I embodied hopelessness, wearing it as if it were my uniform as I desperately struggled to gain the control that I'd never had. The time I was so passionate about saving was the very time I was wasting.

I floundered in that torturous sea for years, my head bobbing up and down, as glimpses of the shores of recovery teased me. It was so hard for me to understand the need to let go. Wouldn't I drown? It felt that way. Each time I binged and purged, the aftermath was the same. My skin would begin to crawl with a familiar, fierce sensation that made my heart pick up speed. I felt as if I were about to lose my mind. It made me want to spit on my own face and punch it unmercifully. But instead, I self-medicated and fed the beast. If I starved, I binged to medicate. If I binged, I purged to medicate. Sometimes I would just lie there bloated, conquered, ashamed, feeling outright insane and out of control—breathing erratically through the residue of anesthetized emotions that threatened to send me crazy forever. In my darkest moments, I would welcome it. Then, the cycle would begin again.

The cycle was the same every time; only the location differed. I would get angry. I would promise myself that I would never do it again. I'd get a day or two of "greatness," where starvation would act as false self-esteem. (One bite of food and it would be all over, of course.) I'd feel better. Then a feeling would come, and I would start emoting. I didn't like it. So once again, I'd act out via my trusted eating disorder behavior. This cycle confirmed that I was saying yes to misery and possible death.

The mental anguish was taking its toll on me. I was beyond tired of a battle that felt unwinnable. For years my battle was about mastering the disorder to ultimately gain control, happiness, and victory. Later it just became about surviving.

This new level of awareness that I was killing myself by choice now slept with me, and when I woke, I was fully conscious while making choices in the eating disorder. It was the same feeling as lying to a loved one's face during an argument. The feeling of being dishonest would stick to my being like unwashed vomit and its smell under my nails after a purge. I was shifting out of denial and into reality.

It was not a particularly special day when I declared defeat. The night before, I had binged on some jarred marshmallow from the dollar store and awoke covered in sweat. I had given myself food poisoning and was vomiting in a friend-of-a-friend's bathroom, someone who had graciously allowed me to stay in her home during my visit to Los Angeles. I had spent my last "dignity dime" on a disorder that promised me the goods of perfection. There, at this generous stranger's home, I slid to the bathroom floor, knowing that without a doubt I had been scammed. Like anyone who has been robbed, I started to review how it could have happened to me.

In a moment of clarity, I understood that I had wanted what the eating disorder was selling. Unfortunately for me, the potion it sold was nothing but candy water disguised as a magic cure. I kept buying what the dodgy salesman in the cheap white suit was selling long after realizing that the goods were bogus. That was my part.

I was twenty-nine, severely depressed, broken, and clueless as to who I really was. I didn't have it in me to muster up that kick-ass energy I believed I needed to begin recovery. I was exhausted. After all, I had been fighting since I was eleven years old. I sat, breathless, in a moment of "oh so familiar."

As I sat next to the toilet, my life through all the years of the disorder played out in my mind scene-by-scene. I didn't try to push the thoughts away or down. Not this time. I was done hiding. I sat still and let it overtake me.

I watched all the different versions I had created of myself appear on the screen of my mind's movie. Me as an actor. Me as a girlfriend, a daughter, a sister. Me as she spat obscenities of self-hate upon any person she loved and trusted, namely her Mum. *What a terrible daughter she was*, I hissed at the screen.

As each scene played out, my mind became quiet. Purging in Australia— cut. Sleeping with random men in Los Angeles—cut. Bingeing in London— cut. Running down the streets drunk in Spain—cut. Looking through the yellow pages for the suicide hotline in Glasgow—cut. Shitting my pants accidentally after consuming bottles of laxatives back in Australia—cut. Promising to myself to be better, do better, as I sat reading the latest fad diet, bingeing *one last time* in all those countries—cut.

The me in the movie looked in the mirror and slapped herself in the face. *She deserves it*, I said to myself, sitting on the bathroom floor of the kind stranger's home. Then the movie began to fade with the me on the screen as alone as I was on the now-warm bathroom tile.

I breathed deeply, aware of the emotions playing tug-of-war between thoughts of taking my own life and the hope for a new one. Just like I did in the cycle of the eating disorder. I knew all the parts in the movie. I wanted a new one.

As I sat on the pink tiles, for the first time in a long time, anxiety had left me. In that calmness, I had a thought that I had never experienced: *What if I said no to the eating disorder? What if I could stop doing what it told me to do? If nothing else, I could do that.* Right there, having calmly stumbled upon my masked truth, a newfound hope blossomed. There was an unexpected shift in me. I had my hands on a simple action I could take. Like a hostage who has no more strength but has the ability to refuse to talk, I was now considering turning *against* the eating disorder and finding the power in saying no to it. I knew how my life looked when I was the "yes-man." I didn't want to do what the eating disorder asked of me anymore, so I said NO. The price, I realized, was way too high. Besides, I was bankrupt.

I so desperately wanted to experience life without the shackles of the eating disorder. I wanted to live, not just survive. The search for perfection—for control—was killing me and honoring no one. I was trying to control something that I never had any power over. All my attempts were futile and full of consequences I could no longer face. There on the kind stranger's bathroom floor, I understood for the first time that I may not be able to control the eating disorder, but I could ignore it. I could walk away. I physically put my hands up with a sense of letting go. I didn't know how I would get to the happiness I longed for, but I realized that the eating disorder wouldn't be the way to get me there either. I had proof of that.

Put the Lid on the Jar of Marshmallows

By Espra

"Liar! You *%#@* liar! You lied to me!"

My stomach dropped, my breath caught in my chest, and I got chills as the core truth of the words hit me. My stomach dropped again when I realized that anyone within a city block must have wondered what lie I had told the woman in my office to bring out such rage.

My first interaction with Robyn involved an angry eruption so deep and heartfelt, the impact was like an explosion detonating behind my office door. Robyn was a self-taught expert on the complex and challenging issues of recovery. She was now on a soul-searching journey to find answers to lingering questions and to still the nagging inner voice that had refused to shut off, even though when I briefly met Robyn she had not engaged in eating disorder behaviors for seven years.

Robyn was forthright about what was on her mind. "I battled the eating disorder for more than a decade, and I have not engaged in eating disorder behaviors for seven years. I no longer allow the eating disorder thoughts to run my life. I am in recovery," she stated proudly, with strength and gratitude. But a part of Robyn also felt haunted. "I know without a doubt that my value and worth do not depend on my weight or size. But still, I have this nagging voice in my head that says they do. I know it makes no sense, but I am struggling to be rid of it." Unfortunately, this made perfect sense to me. These remnants so often cling to the minds of those in recovery, even in the latter stages.

Disgusted by eighteen years of unhealthy thoughts of the eating disorder, Robyn knew not to take them seriously. "I want to tell the eating disorder to leave my head the hell alone," she said. That seemed like a brilliant idea to me, so I initiated an intervention often used in eating disorder treatment: I grabbed a chair, threw a pillow into it, and indicated that it now represented her eating disorder.

"Don't tell me. Tell the eating disorder," I challenged. "Say it with the exact words, intensity, and volume that match how you feel. Don't exaggerate, but don't hold back or filter your words. Don't worry about my naive ears; just tell it what you need to say."

Robyn didn't seem to worry at all about my naive ears as she suddenly clenched her fists and erupted, "Liar! You *%#@* liar! You lied to me!"

Robyn was livid. She was seeing the eating disorder's lies, and she was standing up to them. It was this anger that gave her the strength to set her roots more deeply into her recovery. She was tapping her authentic power instead of relying on the illusion of control offered by an eating disorder. Anger can be scary, yet it gives you the energy needed to push through a barrier that stands in the way of moving toward an important goal in your life. I am not saying that you have to scream or curse in order to stand up to the eating disorder. Do it your own way; just be sure to stand up to it like you mean it.

For the purpose of this book, Robyn and I have chosen to express eating disorder thoughts as if they come from another person. They do not, but these thoughts do come from a different part of our brain than the prefrontal cortex that creates logical thought. The eating disorder thoughts come from the part of the brain that houses emotions, particularly the fear center. Eating disorder thoughts also come from the part of the brain that houses memories of painful events and has tried to make sense of who you are, the world around you, what is safe, and what is unsafe. The eating disorder is an illness that is a part of you (and only a part of you) and is physically located in your brain. That is why eating disorders are called mental illnesses. Technically you do not fight or battle the eating disorder, but rather you work to identify the thought patterns, feelings, urges, and behaviors that over time have led to habits and parts of you that are so strong, clear, and real that they seem to have their own life.

If It Sounds Like an Eating Disorder, Chances Are It Is

Eating Disorder Thought: "Lies, *lies*? These women are crazy. I'm the one who tells you the truth when nobody else will. That's why you need me."

Truth: This statement is just one example of the way an eating disorder's lies can become exhausting mantras. The thoughts are yours (and not to be confused with "hearing voices" or having a separate personality), but they are so clear and powerful, it is like they are their own entity. That's why some people find it helpful to treat their eating disorder thoughts as if they are a distinct or separate persona. Other people work with their eating disorder as if it is a part of their brain, with which other parts of their brain are caught in a tug of war. It is important for you to come to an understanding of the best way for you to conceptualize and work with your own demanding, screaming, or whispering internal eating disorder voice. We will mostly refer to these patterns of thoughts as "the eating disorder." You will get scared as you examine your own eating disorder lies in writing, notice the sheer number of them, and recognize their familiarity. Try hard not to let them scare you away from this journey. Your eating disorder has used these lies to keep you submissive to it, and it will use the same tricks to try to block your path to recovery.

If you struggle with an eating disorder, the following eating disorder quotations will resonate with you in an eerily familiar way. If you do not suffer from an eating disorder yourself, they might make no sense at all. Use the quotations to try and touch the agony of having such brutal and unrelenting thoughts in your head.

Eating disorder thoughts often contain a small strand of truth, around which a tapestry of deceit is woven. You cannot expect to see the deceit until you start to pull away from the disorder's grasp and see the bigger picture. So let my examples of a typical eating disorder voice guide you in becoming more aware of your own.

Consider committing to doing something very different than what you've done in the past. Here's your chance to make a move. Open your mind. Be aware of your eating disorder thoughts and question their accuracy. See if doubt enters your mind. You may just catch the eating disorder in one of its lies.

Recovery Does Not Equal Fat

Eating Disorder Thought: "They are going to try to get you to gain weight, throw away everything you've worked so hard to create, and do that 'accept your body because you are wonderful on the inside' crap! Feeling okay about a fat, gross, and disgusting body will only make matters worse for you."

Truth: Recovery does not mean you will start eating, lose control, gain weight, and never stop. Nor does recovery guarantee that you will not need to go above whatever weight, size, or measurement your eating disorder has imposed on you.

(I'd love to see the eating disorder's book of logic: How does it pick appropriate weight, size, measurement, or intake goals, anyway?) My clients frequently say they could recover if they knew for sure they wouldn't have to gain weight, or wouldn't gain and gain weight and never stop. I wish so badly there was a way to calm this terror before you walk headlong into it. Reassure yourself, if needed, by telling yourself that you are not stuck forever with anything that only brings you misery.

Recovery is about learning who you are and living a life that lines up with your long-term goals and values. You may notice thoughts that you need to get skinny "enough" before you start recovery, that you are too fat to have an eating disorder, or that you are too fat for others to believe you have one. These are eating disorder thoughts, and they are backwards. The eating disorder makes it seem like being skinny enough is the solution that will make everything okay. You must find a way to step back from this belief and see that the eating disorder, not the size or shape of your body, is now the cause of your problems. It keeps you from seeing the actual problems. Perhaps it convinces you that if you could stop bingeing, have more discipline, or just eat less, you would no longer need to purge. And for the record—just in case your eating disorder tells you that purging is only throwing up—purging is any behavior that you use to rid your body of unwanted calories. It can include laxatives, vomiting, exercising, and numerous other behaviors.

It is amazing that you will even consider recovery when you are afraid it will make you have a body that is different than the size and shape that you desperately want it to be. This is a terrifying part of the journey. Both Robyn and I want to be clear that there is no guarantee that you will lose weight or that you won't need to gain weight, depending on your circumstances. I promise that I will teach you how to keep your eating disorder from calling the shots on what is or is not in your body's best interest—and that working on recovery means that we help you find ways to see yourself more as a whole person than an object that is only worthwhile if it looks a certain way.

I guarantee it is possible to learn how to give your body what it needs by eating when you are physically hungry and stopping when you are physically full, most of the time. When you do this, your body will settle into its balanced place. In that balanced place, your body will have the strength and stamina to do the things it needs and wants to do without running out of fuel and without hauling around fuel that it doesn't need. Robyn and I will teach you how to have a new relationship with your body and the food you put in it, and in turn the voice/thoughts of the eating disorder will hold little power.

It Takes as Long as It Takes

Eating Disorder Thought: "Your new job starts in three weeks. By then, if you work hard enough and do this right, you can crank through recovery, get this behind you, and be ready to start your new job and your new life."

Truth: I wish I could give you an estimated "time for arrival" for your recovery, but there truly is no time frame. It takes anywhere from months to years, and the most helpful mindset is that it takes as long as it takes, so stick with it. The reason is, each person has their own lock, and its combination is discovered along the journey. You have to find it, and you will, along the way. Recovery isn't a nice, clear picture of your identity, your passions, or your life's purpose that suddenly shows up one moment. These images start to form while you are busy trying to find them.

It is like having a box that has a picture of a completed puzzle on its front, while you only have a couple of pieces in your hand. You'll need to commit to searching for the other pieces. During your search, a time will come when you look around and see little shimmers of light starting to peek through, revealing parts of the picture that have been created by starting to put together the many pieces of you. Recovery is subtle. If you are working at recovery, please trust that positive changes are happening. You will begin to see glimpses of liberation and peace as you put more and more pieces together.

Take heart from the wisdom of my clients, who often reprimand me when I try to encourage them to use the "one day at a time," principle from twelve-step programs: "One day at a time? Hell, a day is an eternity! It's got to be one minute at a time, and sometimes even one second at a time!" They feel this approach respects the intensity of their personal battle. There's no right or wrong. Do whatever it takes for you to feel supported and encouraged . . . as long as you are not taking direction from your eating disorder. And if you need to take it one second at a time, then do it. *Just stay in the race.*

One way that urgency with time is important, though, is with making commitments and finding ways to stay motivated. Those things cannot wait. Do not sit and wait to feel motivation before you act. Instead, use action as a way to create and sustain motivation. **Action, more often** Then, over time, your actions will change your **than thinking,** feelings in a "fake it till you make it" kind of **creates motivation.** way. This approach works more quickly than trying to change your feelings by first changing your thoughts (although that strategy doesn't hurt, either). One of my colleagues explains this phenomenon by saying, "I am never more motivated to clean my kitchen than after I start to clean my kitchen."

We will continue to remind you that action, more often than thinking, creates motivation. Tough things are easier to put off until tomorrow, with the hope that we will feel stronger motivation by then. Before you know it, another year has passed.

The important thing to know is that people can and do recover from eating disorders. When you stay in the race, you are taking positive steps toward stopping eating disorder behaviors in their tracks. You are then within recovery. It's that simple. And that difficult.

- What commitment are you willing to make right now, regardless of the time involved? You may notice judgments that your commitment is too "dumb" or too "small" to consider. Your commitments must come from you alone, and not from what you think you "should" commit to, or what you think someone else wants. Unless you can make a commitment that is true for you, there will not be enough fuel to sustain you in your journey.

 Think about any commitments, large or small, you are willing to make. Write two of them on a card or in a journal and read them often. Believe me, you will surely need it.

Examples of commitments:
- Get rid of this eating disorder at any cost.
- Read my reasons to recover every day in order to build my willingness to recover.
- Commit to investigating who I am aside from the eating disorder, even though it's scary.
- Decrease binging, restricting, or purging.
- Reduce my self-punishment.

Why Now?

Eating Disorder Thought: "Just get these few pounds off, get this job, and get your career and your relationships on track. You will have what you need to be happy and won't need me after that."

Truth: Why recover now? So you do not lose one more moment of your life! Your eating disorder makes you and those around you miserable, and recovery may be the most difficult battle of your life. So enough! Let's look at the lies, expose the disorder for what it truly is, and get you going toward uncovering "you."

Willpower is your attempt to control the eating disorder. It's helpful, but will only take you so far. You need more. So take a step back (even if you are trembling as you do so), take a stand against your eating disorder, and claim your power. The rest of your life is waiting.

My story may not show on my face.
It may not show in my voice.
But it always shows in my actions.

*Right now, I have the opportunity to start my
day in recovery with my best foot forward.
Right now, I choose to let go of the past and
claim responsibility for my own actions.
I now own my life, my story, and my recovery.*
—Robyn

3.

It's Not About the Food.
And It Is About the Food.

Sunny Days and an Unwanted Houseguest

By Robyn

Some say it is healthy to have some fear and respect for a disorder that can kill you. I had that. I respected that the eating disorder felt like its own identity that went to any lengths to keep me within its clutches. For so many years, I feared I would die a slow death from it—or worse, continue to live as I was—if I didn't do something about it now.

I knew that I had a part in utilizing the eating disorder behavior, that the eating disorder had served me by numbing the intense fear that revved like a motor within and encouraged the anxiety that had plagued me since childhood. The eating disorder was like a guest I'd invited to party at my home on weekends, but who ended up living there permanently, rent-free. Then slowly, quietly it began to dictate my every move. I allowed it to because I needed control, and the eating disorder behavior gave me a false sense of having it.

At the beginning, my guest (the eating disorder) promised me I'd feel better—more at ease in my body—and provided me with ways to feel like I fit in. I welcomed that. Then it turned on me. One morsel of food out of place, one diet screwed, or one drink too many, and it went into a rage. Somehow, we had become a team, and that team had an unbreakable code and an unspoken contract of free residency for the eating disorder at my expense. It was like the character in the movie *Single White Female*—possessing intent to kill. It said no one would like me because I was a fat, lazy loser. It said that I would never amount to anything because I couldn't control myself. It said that no one respects a person who can't look after herself and achieve such a simple task as a perfect weight. It said it was pointless for me to pursue my dreams as an actor. Hell, it said, it's pointless of you to continue living. It coaxed me toward killing myself and saving my loved ones the misery of having to be so disappointed in me. But maybe, just maybe, I would get somewhere if I took its advice, because I knew nothing. I *was* nothing. I knew the eating disorder was right. It was, after all, just telling me what I already deep down believed.

And like in many abusive relationships, I lived with the eating disorder knowing I would do anything it said in order to get and keep my goal weight and attempt to earn self-esteem, respect, peace, and love from others in the process. I needed to be liked because I was too fragile to handle indifference. The eating disorder promised me that I could be everything I wanted. I knew a few years into it that I would never be everything to everyone, but I kept trying anyway.

"This time it will work," it promised me. I knew it wouldn't, but I did it anyway. What else could I do? Sit with myself? Stand up for myself? I didn't have it in me. Besides, I knew I couldn't do it alone. Being thin felt like the only chance I had to start over and begin living my life. It was like buying tickets to win the lottery in order to be able to live in financial abundance, only buying the tickets was making me broke.

If I truly wanted to have recovery, I had to learn to relate to the world, my body, and myself differently.

With all the fear and uncertainty I had for the recovery process, I also found a great amount of willingness and courage in me when I realized that the eating disorder was a liar. I held onto that while committing to myself that I would not die like this, nor continue to live like this. I secretly began to store any evidence of my abusive tenant's behavior. The eating disorder needed to be removed, but I had to be smart about it. I had tried before, and it had failed. It always failed. Now I had to do something different. It was time to take back my home, my body, and if that meant I needed to eat food and sit (as scary as that felt) with it, I would. If it meant eating three meals a day when I wanted to eat none or 1000, I would. If it meant shaking out the rug where I had stored all my emotions for the past eighteen years, I would do that too. Because the truth is whatever I fear is never as bad as I think it will be when I finally walk through it, and if I truly wanted to have recovery, I had to learn to relate to the world, my body, and myself differently. I could do both, be scared *and* do something different—that's recovery.

There is so much more to recovery than the food; it is a mental illness after all. It's not like just saying no or calling the part of the mental illness that felt cruel a liar was enough. Overcoming mental illness takes more than just stopping the behavior, but that's a great place to start. It is hard to recover from an illness if we're abusing our bodies. For this reason, in this book, Espra and I personify the eating disorder. Separating the illness from myself allowed me to build a different relationship with it.

Over the years of my recovery, and as a mental health recovery advocate, I have had the opportunity to train countless people to rebuild a relationship with their body and the food they put in it. I've come to refer to it as *The Body Conversation*. You'll find Espra referring to it as nutritional healing. Wanting recovery and freedom from the obsession of body and food is one thing, learning how to build a new relationship with them is another. There are no quick fixes in eating disorder recovery, and there are no perfect grades to aspire to. I like to think of it as starting a conversation with myself just like I would when meeting someone I am attracted to. I start slowly, with a few coffee dates. Maybe it extends to a dinner date, then first base . . . you get the idea.

When I first started recovery, I wanted so much to be able to eat normally. I wanted to start eating whatever I wanted, whenever I wanted, but I wasn't there yet. Creating a new relationship with food takes time, just as challenging and removing the fear around the food does. I had chosen to stop listening to the eating disorder's lies about body and food, and now I had to stop lying to myself. I had long ago lost the connection with my body's signals. It had been screaming for years, and I chose to ignore it. It would take time to rebuild trust of myself.

I knew if I wanted to have a chance at ending eating disorder behaviors, I would have to find ways to help myself feel safe first. Safety meant providing a structure surrounding food that also allowed some freedom to explore my relationship to it. A structure that would keep me safe mentally, but also help keep the eating disorder's voice quiet (that part of me that felt I needed to control it.) I prepped for the eating disorder's eviction by committing to connect to my body. I started the eviction process by doing the exact opposite of what it would have me do. I started eating three meals a day whether I wanted to or not.

With every meal came a knock at the door from the eating disorder, it wanted to move back in. I ate the three meals anyway, metaphorically closing the door on the eating disorder. I started looking at the behavior of the illness as if it were a vampire. It could not come in if I didn't invite it.

I started walking for forty-five to sixty minutes each day—any more would invite the eating disorder back home. I also stopped drinking alcohol because I had a tendency to replace one crutch with another. You know how I said I had to start learning how to court my body and get to know it slowly? I couldn't do that if I was drinking. Those coffee dates would turn out to be sleepovers before I knew it, and that went against my values. The shame of it would have me back in the clutches of the eating disorder behaviors.

When I was getting into recovery, there were no eating disorder facilities to go to, and even if there were, insurance surely wouldn't have covered it. I was a foreigner, so I scrambled for any kind of available resources that didn't have me needing to return home to Australia.

I also began attending twelve-step meetings to prevent the desire to "switch the witch for the bitch." Just because I was making inroads to recovery didn't mean I didn't have a deep desire to numb my feelings. Drinking alcohol often took the place of my disordered eating in times when my food was "under control." If you can relate, maybe you could consider shelving alcohol for the time being, without judgement or labeling yourself. You can re-evaluate your relationship with it later.

I had done so much research on what the media labeled "good" and "bad" diet foods that I could have taken nutritional exams and passed with flying colors. I had to place all the information I had gathered during the years of chronic dieting aside and commit to starting from scratch. I had to attempt to erase all that I thought I knew and take small steps, steps that were not dictated by the eating disorder, as much as possible. Sometimes it was hard to distinguish the eating disorder's thoughts from mine. But I was learning to sit still and ask for help. And when I knew the next best action to take toward my recovery, only then did I take it.

I tried weighing and measuring my food and found that it triggered me. I tried mindful eating and found that I was ultimately starving myself because my body wasn't creating hunger signals yet. Deprivation meant depression, and my recovery meant not self-imposing mental or physical pain any longer.

When I finally embraced the concept of eating three meals a day, it provided me with a structured freedom that removed much of my shame and guilt. It allowed me, for the first time, to have a say in what I ate, yet also have the structure that I craved so I could begin to listen to my body. I began to make peace with my plate.

It wasn't as if I was letting go of control completely when eating within the structured approach. In fact, when you think about it, there's actual control in having a food plan, and even more control in removing alcohol. The goal in my recovery was not about "losing control." It was about challenging the self-destructive ways in which I was trying to gain it.

During my stay in Los Angeles, I ended up living in the kind stranger's house for three months. Rebecca was in her mid-thirties. She had thick, black hair—the type you would see in a shampoo commercial—with bright blue, almond-shaped eyes. She was a unique, creative woman with a passion to nurture others. Her quirky sense of humor and forthrightness made me feel comfortable and safe during a time I needed it most. I knew where I stood with Rebecca, and I liked that. I needed *that*. Over my short stay at Rebecca's house, she'd become my support person in my early recovery. We all need a Rebecca in our early recovery.

It was summer in Los Angeles, a city where the temperature often reached the high nineties. One morning when walking with Rebecca, I felt my anxiety shift as if the weight of the world was sliding off my shoulders. For the first time in forever, I felt a sense of well-being in my body. Depression was being replaced with a lightness, and I felt present and alert as I walked around Silver Lake taking in a delicious breeze kissing me between my shoulder blades. In that moment, I felt like I didn't have a problem. But just as fast as I had that thought, it was replaced with a sudden urge to protect myself. I sensed danger. I had been here before. Just moments after feeling like I had achieved something, the eating disorder came lurking. Again, I was reminded that I was on a journey of recovery, not yet at my destination.

Many teachers, gurus, and masters who have gone before us say that it is helpful to remember where you came from. I remembered all the pain and numbness, anxiety, depression, disgust, despair . . . along with momentary satisfaction from hitting the "right" number on the scale. I especially had a great sense memory for all those times I was in a relationship and "skinny."

They were experiences that held a powerful sensation that I had "arrived." The feeling was something I equated to becoming a celebrity.

Nonetheless, I was now officially on my recovery journey. I was ready for my houseguest (now trespasser) to stay away. I desperately wanted a new relationship with my body and the food I put in it. The obsession with them both had removed me from life. There was no room for anything else. I wanted to be rid of the eating disorder. After all, here's what the eating disorder had offered me: Reaching my goal weight by eating only apples every day. (This ended in a binge.) Freedom to eat all I desired by purging everything back up. (This resulted in swollen face, scratched throat, bloating, bad breath, and a chronic starving sensation.) Pretending that everything had cigarette ashes or burnt matches in it, because I hated anything to do with smoking, so that I would not want to eat it. Looking in the mirror and telling myself how disgusting I was, and how I would never find a partner that wanted the image I saw in the mirror.

A profound shame would send me into a binge. Sometimes, I would even punch myself in the head. I tried things I never should have enacted upon my body, and I did things that amplified the disrespect and contempt I had for my body and myself. Ultimately, the disorder had left me hopeless, locked in my bedroom alone, calling the suicide hotline; spending six hours at a time staring down at the toilet bowl; roaming dark city streets in search of a gas station so I could get food after a night out drinking. I was defenseless and outright careless when I drank—not caring felt better than feeling. Despite all that I knew about the eating disorder, when the rubber had hit the road and it was time to talk about food, I was petrified.

This time, however, I would not give up on myself. I wanted more of the positive feelings I got a glimpse of as I walked around Silver Lake with Rebecca. I had proof I could have that now. I was ready to rewrite the next scenes of my life, without the eating disorder, or at least without the behavior of it. I felt like there could be a whole new world out there for me—and a whole new world within me too. One where I could feel safe honoring my body, and ultimately, myself.

How to Free Yourself from a Household Pest

By Espra

Right Now It Has to Be About the Food
Eating Disorder Thought: "Sure this tastes good, but you don't deserve it. Well, eat it and enjoy it now that you've started. Just decide how you will make up for losing control."
Truth: Eating disorder recovery is not just about food, but it is impossible to recover when the eating disorder is choosing what, when, and how you eat or what nutrients you keep in your body.

During eating disorder recovery, total abstinence from food is clearly not an option. My clients get extremely frustrated that their eating disorder recovery requires healing their relationship with food, while at the same time having to be exposed to and continue to use the object of their addiction. Whether you battle urges to have more, less, or none at all—you still have to face food and you have to eat, no matter what.

We are talking about stabilizing your nutrition by eating a wide range of foods in adequate portions and on a regular schedule. Robyn realized the necessity of creating safety for her body by eating to give her the mental, emotional, spiritual, and physical strength to overcome the eating disorder. I recommend seeking out a registered dietitian who has knowledge of eating disorder difficulties and a non-dieting approach to recovery. This is the first step toward establishing a new and balanced relationship with your body and the food

For your safety, it is essential that you work with both a physician and a registered dietitian with specialized training and experience in treating eating disorders.

you put and keep in it, to start reversing the eating disorder process. For your safety, it is essential that you work with both a physician and a registered dietitian with specialized training and experience in treating eating disorders. Now you are mobilizing a team of knowledgeable individuals, rather than your eating disorder, to help you with your nutrition.

Without regular nutrition, your body, thinking, emotional resilience, mood, judgment, energy, and motivation all become compromised. You may be unable to see it. I can see the effects of inadequate nutrition when clients regularly ask me to repeat a question I just asked, repeatedly forget what we've discussed, or forget what they have agreed to do. This usually disappears after nutrition is more stable and the brain is fed. Often my clients see the improvement in their thinking and agree (although not always in these words) that "malnutrition makes you stupid." This is one more reason why recovery, at this stage, needs to be about the food.

It is not unusual for clients to tell me that their bodies do not need regular nutrition because they have enough stored fat to keep them alive without eating anything at all for a year. You may notice a similar thought. You may also notice the urge to skip this section because you know as much about nutrition as any professional, and that structuring nutrition is important for others, but not for you. This is a common eating disorder thought. I hear this from clients who are severely underweight, those who have been told by others that they are obese, and all weights in between. It is absolutely not true. *Always* be suspicious when your thoughts say that you are an exception to the rule, because such thoughts are serious eating disorder symptoms. It is a fact that malnutrition can occur at any weight. It is caused by deficits in micronutrients and hydration that cannot be diagnosed based on weight, size, the number of fat rolls you can pinch, or other criteria that you or your eating disorder come up with.

The first tier is the foundation upon which the other two tiers are built.

As part of our work to help you find a recovery strategy, we created, based on Robyn's work, *The Body Conversation*. It is a three-tiered approach. The first tier is the foundation upon which the other two tiers are built. This chapter teaches you about Tier One: The Structured Approach. For now, this is your most important tool as you build a foundation for your entire recovery. Start with the Structured Approach and stick with it until you can do it consistently despite your fear. Resist the urge (and your eating disorder's directive) to skip ahead to the next phase of eating because you "already know this stuff," or because you feel you should be further along, you're bored, you weigh enough anyway, or any other reason your eating disorder can create for doing so.

Tier One: The Structured Approach

Eating Disorder Thought: "You can't eat as much or as often as others." "You are small-boned and need less food than most people." Or "You are big-boned and can't eat as much food as most people." Or "You need to eat less often, not more regularly."

Truth: Notice how cunning the eating disorder thoughts can be? It actually uses opposing arguments to prove the same point, which is that you need to eat less than "normal." You would laugh at me if I tried that! Either way, you might be convinced that structured eating is wrong for you and will make you any other body size than the one you want to be. What the eating disorder doesn't tell you is that metabolism, one of our body's most brilliant survival mechanisms, shuts down without regular nutritional intake, making your body less efficient in using and spending the fuel you put into it.

Perhaps you think (and the eating disorder will be telling you) that you are ready to choose what and when to eat in a way that is free of its directives. Know that your eating disorder is desperate for you to experiment with eating "normally." Then it can convince you that you are eating adequately when you are actually following its mandates instead. To recover, you will need awareness, mental strength, and stamina in order to identify the eating disorder's voice. To fuel these, you need regular nutrition. To be safe, you need to follow a structured eating plan and not a plan of your own (or your eating disorder's) design.

Structured eating is also important because your body and your mind are more than likely unable to send and receive accurate signals about when to eat and what foods you need. Like Robyn, without structure, you enter the eating disorder's life-destroying cycle. Structure moves you away from that cycle. Restricting food makes you feel physically and psychologically deprived. Hunger and deprivation often lead to bingeing. Bingeing leads to purging or increased efforts to restrict. The cycle is vicious, and it is a prescription for hopelessness. For others, they remain in the clutches of constant hunger and restricting nutrition, unable to break free from the panic of the sensations, thoughts, or urges that would allow them to take in the nutritional fuel that the body needs to adequately function.

Your dietitian will recommend regular nutritional intake that includes at least three meals and three snacks per day. Waiting more than three to four hours between meals or snacks can create fluctuations in the body's store of chemicals like serotonin, which gives us a sense of well-being, and blood sugar, which gives us energy. People often report things like "fuzzy" or "foggy" thinking, feeling grumpy, feeling tired, and other symptoms when their nutritional intake is inadequate or too infrequent to properly fuel their body and brain.

Because eating disorders love to use eating between meals as an invitation to binge or to emotionally batter you for eating at all, let me clarify the purpose of snacks. Snacks are small portions of food for the purpose of "topping off" your body's fuel tank to keep you functioning mentally, emotionally, and physically at your best. Sometimes you may feel hungry, sometimes you may feel full. If it isn't your body feeling uncomfortable with this, it will be your mind. That is just the way it is in early recovery. Be prepared to experience and endure these symptoms, as doing so will help to move you physically and mentally toward recovery.

Throwing away ideas of "right" or "wrong," "good" or "bad," or "forbidden" foods, is absolutely in the best interest of your recovery.

Do not let your eating disorder distort my recommendation for topping off your tank by encouraging you to binge or omit eating. Typical snack ideas include jerky, granola bars, fruit, cheese, nuts, yogurt, candy bars, or nut butter. The choices are unlimited, yet you have to make some selections ahead of time to increase the chances of making snacks happen. Your registered dietitian can give you examples of snacks that might work best for you.

Robyn found that each time she kept her commitment to eat a regular snack, she moved a little further from the grips of the eating disorder. Over time she included snacks that felt less safe in order to increase her tolerance for variety, thus further challenging and talking back to the eating disorder. Let us be clear that each time you throw away ideas of "right" or "wrong," "good" or "bad," or "forbidden" foods, it is absolutely in the best interest of your recovery.

We are giving you the strategy Robyn ultimately used to deliberately structure her own nutrition for recovery. Robyn's plan worked best for her because it created a clear boundary for her eating disorder. And although it didn't tell her what she had to eat, it kept the eating disorder contained within its structure while it provided Robyn freedom to make choices of her own. Robyn says this safety net was her "structure for freedom." Robyn used the Structured Approach to guide her food choices for a year. In addition, it was well beyond that year when she actually lost her fear of all foods.

Robyn and I felt there needed to be some kind of tool to help relieve this added burden for those working on their relationship with food as part of their recovery. Building a new relationship with your body and the food you put in it is a vital part of the eating disorder recovery process. Let's face it, recovery is hard enough without having to deal with the old beliefs and concerns about what foods to eat, how to distribute foods, or how to portion them. We consulted government sites and I talked with my registered dietitian colleagues, but we couldn't find a tool that we believe represents the range and freedom of nutritional choices and recommended portions without promoting anti-recovery concepts of "good" or "bad" foods. To visualize this is hard. That's why we designed a visual of it below. Take this tool to a registered dietitian who specializes in treating eating disorders. Ask your dietitian to consider your specific needs and help you customize a structured eating plan that works best for you.

Caution: If you work evenings or nights, there is a high risk that your eating disorder will work to manipulate you by saying that you can't do a normal schedule, so you cannot fit in three meals and three to four snacks per twenty-four-hour period. Do not fall for this deception. It is still possible and it is still necessary for you to restore you mind and body with consistent nutrition.

In her early recovery, Robyn recognized that the eating disorder thoughts, along with anxiety, were heightened due to her starting the recovery process—particularly anything to do with food. Here, Robyn talks about the way she had to approach this tool in order for it to work in her own recovery:

> "One of the things I needed to be conscious of was my willingness to play honestly come meal time. I needed to allow myself permission to eat what I felt like, filling the plate without judgment. I had to continually remind myself why I had the plate and not to abuse, manipulate, or make up a story of why I didn't have to stick to the structure. Piling food on the plate was as dishonest as not filling it."

 Use your own structured food plan that you and your registered dietitian create. Make a one-day sample schedule of how you might structure your own eating plan for recovery. For your food plan to have the best chance of being helpful, don't plan breakfast at seven if you get up at ten. Plan on your first meal of the day within one to two hours of waking up, no matter what time that is. Allow your times to vary if needed, but most importantly practice your structured food plan with realistic expectations of yourself, while also pushing enough so your eating disorder doesn't call the shots. This is about successful steps toward your recovery. When your eating disorder screams at you, locate your reasons to recover that you wrote down from Chapter One.

Example:

Time	Helpful Hints
Breakfast 7:30 a.m.	Be flexible: If you wake up at 9:30 a.m., eat your breakfast then. Remember to eat three meals a day. Don't let eating disorder thoughts convince you into starting your day with a snack, then only fitting in two meals. Any form of deprivation will set us up to fail.
Snack 10:00 a.m.	If you can, set your snack time for a regular work or class break. Otherwise, problem-solve how you can set aside ten to fifteen minutes to eat, even if to start it is on-the-go.
Lunch 1:00 p.m.	Again, be flexible, and be sure to eat a meal (as outlined within the diagram,) not a snack.
Snack 3:30 p.m.	To help set you up for success, consider choosing foods that are highly portable to be accessible during some snack times.
Dinner 7:00 p.m.	Nighttime is a high-risk time for bingeing or restricting! Freedom: You don't have to hide because of eating disorder behavior anymore. If this is a high-risk time for you, initially structure where and when you prepare and eat your meal. It is less likely that you will engage in eating disorder behaviors if you are not alone *and* if you have kept up with your structured eating throughout the day.
Snack 9:30 p.m.	Freedom: Most individuals are hungry before bed. Having a snack now defies both the eating disorder rules and a common rule for many dieters that "you can't eat after a certain time of day." Eat a snack anyway.

Most of our lives interfere and leave insufficient time, energy, and willingness to remain committed to structured eating. Whether you are working at recovery or just trying to manage your nutrition as well as possible while living life in this crazy world, structured eating is a challenge for nearly all of us. Even long into recovery this approach provides us with optimum health—both physically and mentally.

Variety Is the Key

Eating Disorder Thought: "Variety. That's a bunch of crap. The first bite of cheesecake you add to their *variety* plan will blow everything because you will lose control and never stop eating. The structure you really need is self-discipline, not to be fooled by some structured eating trick."

Truth: Eating a variety of foods creates fuel that your body and brain need to maximize their capabilities.

Robyn included grains, fruits and vegetables, protein, and fats in every meal. This is necessary for healing, and it will automatically happen when you increase your range of foods. This also helps fuel your spirit, as each time you refuse to let the eating disorder decide what you will and won't eat, the less power it has over you.

Creating boundaries for your eating disorder is a large part of the formula to decrease its control over you. A vital function of working with a dietitian is to help you identify and normalize foods that trigger your eating disorder behaviors, like those you fear and avoid as well as those you embrace and consume excessively or in an unbalanced way. Simultaneously, you must create freedom for yourself, so that neither you nor your eating disorder feels totally controlled or totally out of control. The force of will you expend trying to control your eating disorder through willpower alone is admirable, but burns a lot of mental and emotional energy, with limited and short-lived results. Save some energy for problem-solving and for the persistent readjustments to keep your behaviors on target.

Control, when used by itself and without a clearly defined, objective plan, causes you to end up pushing against the eating disorder that can feel as if it is pushing back even harder. In the big picture, it gets you nowhere. The freedom that you are seeking is the true power that is buried deep within you. Structured eating will help you begin to uncover and gather the pieces of that power as you define your own preferences rather than being controlled by those of the eating disorder, or those of anybody outside of your chosen eating disorder supporters. Whether you are rigid or experimental at certain times is your choice. Just make sure you do not persistently default to rigid. And you win either way, because you either challenge an eating disorder food rule or you challenge rigidity by making your own choice.

Inside of these boundaries, Robyn's freedom came through being able to make her own choices. Robyn allowed herself to sometimes choose what the eating disorder thoughts considered extremes because she knew either way she was still within the structure, but also challenged herself to choose from a middle path between the extremes—the place of unlimited possibilities that she never usually visited with the eating disorder. If she felt particularly frightened, instead of skipping the meal due to fear, she went with foods that felt safer (rice instead of a donut, for instance). When she felt more liberated or needed to push herself to challenge the eating disorder "rules," she went with food choices that felt more risky or rebellious (like fried chicken). It was necessary for her to do both. It was her choice, and that was important to her, as it is to all of us. That is freedom. That is recovery.

 What practical issues might get in the way of your structured food plan working? Make a list of these. For example, perhaps you work a night shift some nights that requires eating dinner at 7:00 a.m., or maybe you have nowhere to store food during the day. Think of ways to solve the problems that might get in the way. Then write the solution you choose. Use it, and see if it works. If it works, good. If not, try another solution (and then another) until you find one that does work. Make a list of available foods to eat at those times. (Don't forget about the portable foods that are sometimes necessary.) Other examples of issues that might need problem-solving include forgetting to eat, forgetting to take food from home or not having food with you when you need it.

There is freedom for creativity here, and I have seen amazingly creative solutions. For example, 1) Both Robyn and I have

difficulty eating solid foods early in the morning. We both drink smoothies and shakes (not low-calorie or those designed for weight loss) that combine all food categories from the plate for breakfast (not *every* meal). 2) Sometime activities get in the way of lunch: Honor your lifestyle. Set a lunchtime alarm on the phone; keep durable and portable foods in a bag, backpack, or your car so you can eat something no matter what.

Exercise

Eating Disorder Thought: "Your body needs at least three hours of intense exercise a day or you'll be out of shape."

Truth: Exercise is to eating disorder recovery as fertilizer is to rose bushes. The right amount is helpful and too much is deadly. The right times and amounts of application are determined by specific criteria, not by how you feel (or instructions offered by an eating disorder).

Robyn limited herself to thirty minutes per day of exercise, as that approach worked well for her recovery. **It is important to talk with your physician and registered dietitian to determine how intensely and how long you should work out, as well as what types of exercise are safe for you. Ask your physician to tell you of any symptoms that might indicate you need to stop your exercise immediately. Follow your doctor's orders. Your eating disorder is not a doctor!**

Absolutely refrain from any exercise that is driven by your eating disorder's need to burn calories, punish you, or control your activity in any other way.

Listen closely so you can catch your eating disorder's attempts to be in charge of this. If you find yourself arguing that there is a reason you should be doing more, know that this voice is most likely your eating disorder. Take a deep breath, clear your mind, and renegotiate your physician's and registered dietitian's guidelines with them as professionals, not with your eating disorder. For those who are inactive, it is important for you to safely add physical activity, as it decreases your vulnerability as well.

Think of a physical goal that you want to work toward that is within the boundaries your healthcare providers have set for you. Then choose two physical activities that will help you work toward that goal. The best way to balance exercise for your recovery is to focus on "fun" activity goals.

Healing nutritionally is the foundation upon which the rest of your recovery will be built. Do what you need to do, not because you are fearless, but because you refuse to let fear dictate your life.

For life is good here where I stand.
I am safe here where I stand.
And there is no need for eating disorder,
here where my feet meet the ground.

*It is safe for you to trust that you can and will
have a better life without the eating disorder.
Today, put your trust in a new way of life where
your body, mind, and soul are nurtured, where you
look and feel your best—it's called recovery.*
—Robyn

4.

Learning to Hit Curveballs

Avalanches and the Bogeyman Within

By Robyn

One at a time, I took in the taste and texture of the eucalyptus drop, and each time my tongue rolled over the hardened lump, memories of childhood life oozed out, along with the sweetness of sugar and sharpness of eucalyptus. My brother Anton sent me a care package the other day filled with my favorite lollies. I felt like a little kid again. Yes, I still get giddy at the sight of my favorite candy. With the care package came a sense of opening up a treasure box of all the past events that made me who I am today. I find myself in curiosity now, instead of pain and regret, but still trying to connect the dots of my story, as if I may now, after all this recovery, be able to discover the exact reasoning behind my circumstances.

Having had my own children, I know they were born with their own temperaments. Their temperaments and experiences are the very things that shape their personalities and how they respond to the world. That is true for me too.

I came from an incredibly loving family. My parents, at times, suffocated me with love—hugging me and kissing on me daily, just like I now do with my girls. My mum was always there for me, except for when she physically couldn't be. Mum was an intellect. So smart and so loving. She didn't yell at me like I sometimes do with my girls. She had the softest of hands, that when they held me, I felt safe—like *really* safe. She was deep breathing to anxiety. Her giggle was contagious. It will forever be imprinted in my heart. Both my parents supported my dreams. They worked hard to pay for all my lessons and set me up for success the best way they knew how.

My dad is a good man. Just like Mum had, Dad possesses a beautiful heart, and where Mum had physical ailments, he had mental ones. Until seventy years old, you could have found Dad on the highways between Sydney and Queensland, thinking and dreaming as he hummed along in his semitrailer, trying to get to the next location as fast as possible. Like many men of his generation, Dad found worth as a father providing for his family and took on the screwed-up social belief of his time that weakness was found in talking about his issues, especially if they were of the mental variety. So when I was growing up, he never spoke about his issues, not to a professional, anyway.

When Mum became ill with lupus, life stopped. My young brain searched for answers, as suddenly my ever-present mum was now behind closed doors, bedridden and struggling to stay alive. Where there was once very little privacy in our home—I could often be found sitting on the toilet talking to my mum as she showered—there were closed bedroom doors. The closed doors scared me way more than a threat of a bar of soap after I swore. Us kids understood Mum's bedroom door was closed for a reason, though. We knew that Mum was busy willing her body to live. And yet, without my mum readily available, I was left to deal with the fear of her possible death alone. I made up scary, what-if stories. I didn't know how to soothe myself without her.

All of us in the family dealt with the change of our life so differently. My sister, Betty, left home before Mum became ill. She left at sixteen, was married by eighteen, and gave birth to her first child three months before her nineteenth birthday, so, busy tending to her new family, she wasn't around a ton. With a large age difference, we didn't speak much about what was going on either.

It was my relationship with my brother, Anton, that helped me cope with the emotional upheavals. One night, as we lay in our beds in the darkness, I said to my brother, "Okay, if Mum and Dad separate, you go with Dad and look after him, and I'll go with Mum and look after her. Promise?"

"Shut up, Rob," he said. But he heard me. I know he did. He always had my back; we didn't need to speak about it.

Many afternoons during that time, I experienced glimpses of feeling valued and worthwhile as I aided my big brother in the concoction of mindless boy games. I loved to hang out with him and his friends. Anton is twenty months older than me. I was grateful to be his trustworthy assistant among his popular friends because I was unpopular, teased, and called "chubby" by my peers. I forgot about the possibility of losing Mum, even if only for a short time, when I joined in on his riffraff. As I dealt with the anxiety within by eating, Anton dealt with it by not dealing with it.

And yet there came a time when, even while eating, there was little escape from my feelings. Over time, my emotions would blindside me like an avalanche. Without my even being aware, my thoughts would gain momentum, and my body would be caught in a whirlwind of sheer panic, sobs of desperation, and the sensation that I was the thing that was so very wrong.

Not able to deal with the emotions, I was left feeling out of control. I would try to get back in my body and fight the anxiety, but as with any avalanche, fighting was useless. My emotions had already buried me. Over the years, I have learned that once someone has reached a state of panic, we can no longer reverse it. However, fighting it is the opposite thing one should do. Fighting it makes the panic worse and perpetuates the need for disordered eating. My friend and therapist colleague Lara Effand says: "Panic is like a tidal wave that can become a force that feels like it is swallowing us whole. The more we fight it, avoid it, push it down, the more it controls us. To successfully manage panic, we have to learn how to surf the wave. Accepting it for its power and energy and learning how to rein in the power to gain back our footing and ability to cope."

These days, I have more coping skills available to me, and I am able to read the signs of a potential avalanche. Knowing the signs has allowed me to take action sooner to regulate my emotions. I can slow down, breathe, and ask myself if it's "a snake or a stick." This helps considerably, most of the time.

It doesn't mean that recovery has ended all of my roller-coaster emotions or anxiety. I still feel very deeply, and sometimes that feels wonderful; but when it doesn't, and I don't want to be a part of it, I still try to run. And, like always, the running creates a snowball, and even after all of these years of recovery, I find myself buried in an avalanche of emotions. It is only when I allow myself to feel the discomfort of rising emotions—when I don't run, but instead pause—that I get the opportunity to rewrite my relationship with my emotions.

It is only when I allow myself to feel the discomfort of rising emotions—when I don't run, but instead pause—that I get the opportunity to rewrite my relationship with my emotions.

◆ ◆ ◆

I met my husband, Tim, through a mutual friend in substance use disorder recovery. I had determined that quitting alcohol *first* was what I needed to find long-term recovery from the eating disorder. I chose to give up alcohol because whenever I drank, it felt as if I was hitting a "f*ck it" button, and any recovery momentum I gained before picking up a glass of Chardonnay went out the window, and ultimately prevented me from fully embracing the person I longed to be—someone living in recovery without feeling as if I had to numb my feelings. The bottom line: When I drank, I would either go home with a man or a bag of food. In either case, the "mornings after" were rarely welcomed. Drinking a nice chilled glass of wine gave me a similar high as getting on the scale and seeing I had lost weight through disordered means. I have heard many stories of others with eating disorders who did not need to stop drinking alcohol, and their recovery is full.

It has never sat well with me to call myself an alcoholic. It's not that I'm in denial about the way alcohol affects me or affected my family for generations. Nor is it because I have experienced and also witness others experiencing great shame associated with the unfair "addict" or the "mentally ill" title ignorant people throw around to justify some criminal or malicious act. I immensely oppose claiming any such label or such definition as my own. Labels are for handbags, not human beings. Not only does my gut respond negatively to such socially constructed narratives, I also find that when one buys into such concepts, it is reiterated that those of us who struggle with such illnesses can't be trusted. That we are powerless in all our affairs. Hand on heart, *f*ck that*.

I have spent much of my life feeling unempowered and unsafe with my anxious mind. I didn't want recovery if that's what it looked like. Recovery and freedom represented having choices, having a say. Recovery symbolizes reclaiming my ability to use my voice and define myself.

When in the eating disorder, restriction always felt safe until the need to rebel broke through. As much as I despise labels, it is also true that it is my nature to want to label and put things in their place, to organize things perfectly, and then *boom*. Blow them up. Like an immaculate walk-in closet I've spent days cleaning, and then if one thing is out of place, I tear that shit up. I go from type A to type what the f*ck? real fast. It doesn't happen immediately, of course. It's like one piece of clothing at a time comes loose on the hanger and lies on the wardrobe floor. "I'll pick it up later,"

I say to myself. Then one more and one more, until most of my clothes are now covering the floor rather than the hangers. That's what alcohol did to the eating disorder recovery—it blew it up. That simple, really. No other analysis needed.

In the fall of 2002, I had just returned home from Glasgow, Scotland to Sydney, Australia, having completed my master's degree in solo performance. I had spent some time "sober," and in turn, I was able to maintain five weeks of behavior-free recovery from the eating disorder. I had decided to return to Los Angeles for the upcoming pilot season. One of my childhood friends called me and told me she was having her thirtieth birthday. She had just moved to Northern California and suggested I stop over there to visit and join in the birthday celebrations before heading to Los Angeles. I thought it would be a great way to start my trip.

The day I landed in Oakland, we headed out in the late afternoon for dinner at some fancy-pants bar in downtown San Francisco. I had pushed and prodded myself into my friend's pair of jeans that she'd lent me. They were two sizes too small for me, but I forced myself into them anyway and shuffled into the bar. Moments later, I was introduced to my friend's husband's best friend. A handsome man whom, I confess, I had seen photos of already when my childhood friend visited Australia. From the photos and my imagination, I had already had a love affair with the very inebriated, hot guy now standing in front of me. During my twenties, if you put me in a room with alcohol and a good-looking guy, all commitments to my values were off the table. Needless to say, I got outright drunk that night, and rather than going home with a bag of food, I went home with him. I continued that behavior nightly until blackout and until I was asked to leave the day of my childhood friend's birthday. With our fourteen-year friendship in ruins, I was depressed and feeling broken by the realization of what I'd done. I got on a plane to Los Angeles, and the eating disorder followed me.

Yet, despite my frustration about the antiquated labels spinning around our society and the debate of "Am I?" or "Aren't I?" an alcoholic, I knew the only thing that mattered was getting space between me and the eating disorder behavior. My unhealthy relationship with alcohol seemed to be the glaring difference that got in the way of my recovery process and added up to an eating disorder relapse totaling seven years. So, I decided to look at giving up alcohol not as a label or life sentence, but rather one more tool in the kit toward my recovery.

Coming to the decision to embrace the elimination of mind-altering substances without trying to box myself in has made the overwhelming sense of powerlessness in the disorder so powerful in recovery. Being honest with myself, and owning my truth, has made all the difference between staying stuck and moving forward into life.

◆ ◆ ◆

My decision to abstain from alcohol in the early process of recovery led me to meeting Tim. Being a foreigner with no health insurance (not that it would have helped me back then because no health insurance was accepted in exchange for treatment), and with no other options of support in sight, I attended twelve-step meetings for my unhealthy relationship with alcohol.

Each time I called myself an "alcoholic," I felt as if I was lying to myself. Each time I said I was "powerless," I felt as if I was not honoring that part of me that could be trusted. That part of me that was still there, within me, but just needed help finding. Looking back, I believe it was my need to feel like I wasn't alone, my need for rules to feel safe, and my profound need to restore my faith that I once had as a little girl that led me to the support groups such as the twelve-step meetings. They gave me all of that, including Tim.

I spotted Tim from across the room. It was August 2002. He held an air about himself that was different from all the other men I had once been attracted to. I won't lie though, he was gorgeous, and that was the first thing that caught my eye. He wore a baseball cap, blue jeans, and a black V-neck tee. There was both compassion and strength in his delicious blue-green eyes. He was nine years my senior with wit, humor, charisma, and looks that made me drool. I fell profoundly in love. Okay, lust. But soon after, love.

My relationship with Tim has been one of my biggest teachers in my recovery. Both Tim and I are incredibly passionate, and yes, at times, intense (another label I used to despise but have come to own) individuals in recovery. When we argue, I can still manage to become as confused as that little girl struggling to understand her emotions as I faced my mother's closed bedroom door. The need to fix the problem so I could get out of the discomfort has led me to further avalanches I might have bypassed had I paused, taken a breath, and really grasped what was going on.

Tim used to travel out of state for work a lot. As a family coach and interventionist, he helps families intervene with their loved ones who are struggling with substance use disorder to get into treatment, and later helps integrate them into their home life after treatment. In the earlier years of our marriage and when our girls were young, he would also work as a companion, staying close by the family and loved one's home for hands-on support—for those who had the luxury of affording it. With our girls getting older, they began to recognize their dad's absence, and he theirs, so we'd Skype each night he was away.

One night, just before I called the girls over to talk to Tim at the computer, I told him about my day. I was excited, ignoring his low and drained energy, as I told him about the white trestle I had purchased online to use to hold up an old door that I had refurbished and placed a glass panel on top of it to form a desk. I thought I only needed one trestle to go under the middle of the door, so when Tim asked me if I had purchased an additional trestle to go on the other end of it, I said no. Through my computer screen, I witnessed Tim scrunch up his face with what I perceived as a look of judgment, one that I had seen many times before and had come to loathe. "What do you mean, you didn't buy two of them?" he said. I felt stupid—and angry. I was baffled by his reaction and also by the new awareness that I would, in fact, require *two* trestles, and the interaction quickly became uncomfortable. I asked Tim to stop speaking to me as he was, and he told me I was being defensive. I recognized in that moment that it was his emotions that were stronger than the situation warranted. With this clarity, I was able to react with a calm voice, without escalating the situation. The fact was, he was lonely (missing his girls painfully) and tired, which appeared to influence his interaction with me, and I recognized this. My choices were to engage anyway or step back for a while. *That time* I chose to step back.

For the record, I usually would have yelled back at Tim, defending myself with a vengeance. Whenever a conflict arises, my default is to feel challenged and then become reactive. But on that day, I simply got off the computer without cursing and sat with my girls on the sofa as they watched TV. I sorted through all my emotions until I reached my truth, wading through the usual feeling of worthlessness.

In my recovery, I am learning to recognize when I have spoken or acted in a way that I am not okay with; I get a sense in my gut that tells me so. I didn't get that feeling on that night. In my stillness, I got a sense that Tim already had hard feelings hitting him that were separate from me. Although his words were directed at me, I was clear it was not all about me and the missing trestle.

We are human. It's something I forget all the time—still. Especially when my emotions are high. Sitting without fixing anything is my life lesson. As I sat on the sofa with my girls, watching the film *Nanny McPhee*, I started thinking about the way I left it with Tim. *I'm being too harsh; maybe I should just ask him what's really going on.* I interrupted my thoughts. No, I told myself. *Allow it to just be; give it space, Robyn.* That night each time my need to want to fix Tim and I came about, I reminded myself to breathe and cuddle up with my daughters instead.

Over the years within my recovery, I've learned that my feelings won't kill me. If I sit with my intense emotions, they will not swallow me up, make me go crazy, or cause something catastrophic to happen to me or the people I fiercely love. It turns out that my reactions are the bogeyman in my mind. It is not that I am broken.

In recovery, I got to change my lifestyle by facing the pain I have based many of my decisions, behaviors, and reactions on, and find another way that betters my life and the lives of those around me.

Yes, eating disorders are mental disorders, and yes, they can feel like you're in a battle you just can't win. But we are powerful too. We have feelings that are worthy of being heard, and we can make hard choices that lead us back to the life we were born to live. One that is simpler, more hopeful, and worth fighting for, or surrendering to (depending how you look at it).

What to Do When the Bogeyman Jumps Out

By Espra

Eating Disorders Love Curveballs
Eating Disorder Thought: "You blew that one. You really can't handle anything, can you? You're lucky I'm here. At least there's hope for you to be competent at something."
Truth: The anesthetic benefits of compulsive behaviors wear off quickly and your emotions flood back with a renewed vengeance. Nothing about this devastating pattern helps you learn to cope better. It only makes you better at using eating disorder behaviors.

You probably already feel vulnerable, maybe even fragile and out of control, due to the river of emotions that floods through you. Then life throws you a surprise, good or bad, that you didn't see coming and the eating disorder tells you that you cannot handle it or that you are defective because you handled it "wrong." You are convinced that others have an easier time handling difficulties or handle things well and that something is wrong with you when it doesn't go perfectly. Do you see the distortion? No matter how you handle life's curveballs, when ruled by the eating disorder you risk becoming racked with even more guilt, shame, and fear than before.

Brain science now shows us that self-punishing thoughts all by themselves activate the threat defense system in our brain that urges our body to run, fight, or freeze. We label this anxiety. As eating disorders survive and thrive on self-punishment, the resulting anxiety mandates that you turn back to the eating disorder to "treat" the ever-increasing pain, now caused by the self-punishing activity of your mind.

How do you cope with emotions that are so intensely painful that it seems they will consume you? The eating disorder will likely tell you that you are crazy or weak because you feel such pain and then readily hand you a solution. The distractions and numbing delivered through eating disorder behaviors make it seem like you have hacked into the perfect solutions for coping with pain. But they keep you at the mercy of the same destructive disorder that is threatening your long-term peace and happiness.

The key to increasing your ability to cope with life's curveballs is—just as Robyn did in her interaction with Tim—to be mindful or aware of what is happening. Your emotions will take over your thoughts and actions automatically in situations like this, so your task is to learn and to practice paying attention to what is happening both around you as well as inside of you. Notice when your thoughts or feelings seem impulsive and reactive. This moment is a miracle moment because you have a choice. You will get blindsided because you are a human being with a human brain. Your job is to learn to recognize when you are what I now call "emotionally hijacked" and push pause while you work to decrease the intensity of your emotions and get your thinking brain back on track.

By paying attention, Robyn recognized that she felt blindsided by her emotions in reaction to Tim's words and tone of voice. Robyn's automatic thoughts and physical sensations warned her that her all-too-familiar avalanche of shame, fear, and anger was coming toward her with dizzying speed and force. Of course it mattered that Robyn felt and honored the sting of the pain she felt from Tim's words. And it mattered that Robyn quickly pushed pause and did something different before her hijacked emotions rather than her values and life goals dictated her response to Tim. Robyn exited the conversation (she insists that she didn't even use the "f" word) to allow her intense emotions, physical sensations, and thoughts to settle. It was only after her pause that Robyn could see her "I deserved that" thoughts as more of a byproduct of her shame than a fact.

Robyn knew it was important to pause, both physically and mentally, putting her focus elsewhere and simply breathing for the night. If Robyn had mentally continued the conversation with Tim during her "pause," her emotions would have grown stronger. Instead of helping, the pause would have merely delayed her giving Tim an earful. Always remember, the heart of pausing is to get your attention *away* from obsessing and ruminating about the situation by placing your full attention on what you are doing in the moment. The purpose for pausing is not to ignore or dishonor your feelings. That is dangerous. Pausing is about creating enough space from the situation to keep your emotions from making the decisions about how you act, robbing you of your own choices and authentic control.

Only through years of working to build her ability to pause and find ways to respect and work with her emotions has Robyn come to learn that she can coexist with her intense feelings without ignoring them or clinging to them. She now knows that they, although sometimes very painful, won't kill her. Only then, armed with the authentic power that accompanies stepping into our values and life goals, could Robyn decide how to deal with the situation in a way that maintained her self-respect by honoring her feelings as well as her needs.

It is when you are not aware that emotions are dictating your thoughts and behaviors that you can quickly strike out; foul things up; and get thrown out of places, situations, and relationships altogether (including any relationship you have with yourself). This creates a severe shame storm that will suck you in like a black hole.

Most of my clients with eating disorders fantasize, obsess, and act on eating disorder thoughts and urges as their way of "pushing pause." This is not pausing, it is shutting down and numbing, like a "freeze" reaction to danger. Unlike with electronics shutting down, your brain does not reset itself, and when you have an eating disorder, your default settings are obsessing about your body, food, eating, not eating, exercise, purging, counting calories, and (fill in the blank).

Obsessing left alone leads to cravings that lead to action. For example, many of my clients find themselves standing in front of a mirror, staring and poking at their bodies with disgust, more frequently and for longer periods of time when they are already upset. These are the times when you might find yourself not caring about recovery at all, much less your reasons for pursuing recovery. To navigate intense emotions, a deliberate, non-eating-disordered pause is needed. This chapter is devoted to teaching you how to pause and ride the wave of intense emotions so you don't accidentally make matters worse.

Curveballs Catch Us All Off Guard

Eating Disorder Thought: "Of course Robyn could push pause. She is strong and able to do it. You, on the other hand, are weak and will never be able to manage big emotions."

Truth: Some emotions are painful, and human brains are wired to avoid pain by any means possible. Learning not to unnecessarily add to pain or make things worse by trying to avoid pain is difficult, and you can learn to do it some of the time and eventually much of the time. With time and practice you will build faith that you can ride the wave of painful emotions without having to numb, engage in eating disorder behaviors, or batter yourself. Even if a problem cannot be solved right now, you can learn to ride the wave of emotion without acting on it. You can respect, coexist, and get curious about the nature of your emotions, both those you like and those you dislike.

I don't know much about baseball. I do know that sometimes it seems like everything in our lives is a curveball—elusive, taunting us, confusing, and out of our reach. We think we've got it figured out, then it changes its course and seems to get the best of us. Being in recovery doesn't change the nature of life or end the frustration. Suffering is a human condition, not—as the eating disorder would have you believe—an affliction reserved for "unworthy, undisciplined, fat people who are disgusting and need to be punished" (these are eating disorder words, not mine). Sometimes we can see curveballs coming, but most of the time we cannot. Recovery means you work to find ways to navigate and evaluate situations, thoughts, emotions, and urges rather than numbing, blindly obeying them, or trying to pretend they don't exist.

Somehow, you have got to figure out how to survive curveballs without running to an eating disorder or other addictive behaviors. You also have to learn how to refrain from living as if everything that comes your way will make you strike out. You need protective measures that will not take you out of the batter's box or remove you from the game altogether. Sometimes we all need to take a time out for a breather and to clear our minds; then return to the game and do our best to muddle through, even if we are sure we've already lost. That's the way we all have to do it. Stay in the game. That's a big part of recovery.

Keep in mind that individuals with eating disorders are biologically predisposed to high levels of emotional sensitivity, thus more intense emotional responses than others (but not everyone) around them. This sensitivity is of great worth, yet until learning to navigate it can feel like a curse. Take a sensitive soul, deprive it of resiliency tools for navigating emotional pain and confusion (most of us have not been taught how to manage emotions), and you have a perfect setup for a person to stay in the dugout or not even show up for the game of life. The good news is that with a good set of tools, time, and practice, learning to keep emotions more steady in order to hit the curveballs is possible.

Keep Your Eye on the Ball
Eating Disorder Thought: "Exactly. If you keep your focus on me there's no way you can go wrong."
Truth: When you keep your eye on eating disorder thoughts and behaviors, you can't miss what they drive you to see. But you will miss seeing those things around you that you most desperately want in your life.

I hope you made a list in Chapter One of your reasons to recover and the harm of embracing your eating disorder, even in difficult times. Sorry. Recovery won't happen if you bargain that taking the eating disorder out of the closet to get you through hard times and tucking it neatly away when things are smooth is good enough. Commit to reading your list when things get hard and *before* you act. Reading your list will help you push pause and take a step back.

Respect What Is
In order to face extremely difficult emotions without running for the distraction or illusion of control found in obsessive thoughts and addictive behaviors, you must first acknowledge that something has happened and that you are suffering because of it. You might want it to be different, but you must respect that in that moment it is not the way you want it to be. I am not pushing you to like what is happening, be happy about it, think happy thoughts, say things are okay, or stop hoping or working for change. Genuine

acceptance is the first step in seeing and responding to a situation as it actually is. Otherwise you might gather a hose to fight a fire when it is a flood that is threatening your house.

It helps to come up with a meaningful statement that helps get your mind focused on first accepting that a difficult situation has shown up. I teach my clients a three-sentence approach to help with this:

I want_____. I wish I had _____. But right now I don't. So what am I going to do with that? For example: *I want that one true person in my life who loves me. I wish I had that one true person in my life who loves me. But right now, I don't. So what am I going to do with that?*

One of my clients told me this set of statements "drops me right into validating my wants, my wishes, and respecting and accepting that what I've got in this moment is something different that what I want. Bam, it drops me right into looking at what I need to do with what is actually happening in my world right now. It's like then I can do something useful." If not with this statement, create some phrase of your own to help pull your mind away from how things "should" be, or who is to blame, and toward respecting what is actually happening. Only then can you decide how to effectively approach it.

 What statement can you create that is meaningful to you, and that will help you respect what has shown up for you? Will you work with one of those above or find another one that resonates for you? Write it down. Commit it to memory.

After you drop yourself into the reality of what is going on and that things are different than how you want them, you have to carry that acceptance forward. Warning: Reading this information and saying your statement one time does not glue you to your acceptance decision. You will need to repeat it over and over, you will need to affirm your statement, take a deep breath, let it out, relax your body, uncross your arms, relax your hands, and turn your palms up in a gesture of allowing in information beyond what is rocking around in your mind and body. As you open your body, remind yourself of your decision to respect and work effectively with what this moment has brought to you. Be kind; brains don't like bullies, even if it is you bullying yourself.

Your alternative is to cross your arms, furrow your brow, clench your fists, stomp your feet, and say the eating disorder's favorite words: "I won't (or I can't)." We tend to do this when things are not going our way. Refusing to tolerate pain when things are not going our way is much easier than working to respect and accept the reality; however, it gets in the way of getting through the difficulty with a sense of dignity and self-respect. It gets in the way of recovery.

Be prepared to use your statement as your path to return your mind again and again to your decision to accept instead of push away what is presenting itself to you in the moment. Then gather information so you can decide the most helpful next step. Practice, repeat, and don't expect to perfect this process. It is in the mere practice of reminding ourselves of our ultimate choice, our intention, to accept one difficult moment at a time and repeatedly reopening our body and mind to the intention of that misery. Over time, it can become less miserable more often.

Body Mechanics

Once you've decided to tolerate hard emotions long enough to keep yourself from doing the things that will make matters worse in the long run, you can begin using other skills to help you ride out emotional and behavioral urges instead of acting on them. Although it might feel that without an outlet, the urges will continue to build forever—believe it or not, these emotions and urges eventually decrease if you don't act on them. It will be difficult for you to believe that right now, so please trust me. The only way to build faith in this is to give it a good, honest, lengthy try for yourself and see what you notice.

Because turning to behaviors that quickly numb emotion brings significant relief immediately, it sets up a powerful reinforcement cycle that is difficult to break. The package is wrapped so attractively that it is tough to resist. For more peace in the long-term, please work hard to resist it anyway.

Tolerating pain by using skills, on the other hand, takes more time and effort but helps you forego the behaviors that make matters worse. You may not feel better or relieved. Learning to tolerate the pain helps decrease your chances of running to eating disorder behaviors in a panic. In the long run, you will see the benefits of using coping skills over numbing your mind. My clients appreciate the sense of pride, authentic power, and self-respect that emerge from those deeper places within as they practice over time. Stick with it.

This is a dangerous time to let your emotions have their way. Take some time for the dust to settle. Give yourself time to look at the situation you are in with eyes and a mind that are curious, open, and able to take in new information. This sort of mindful, aware, and awake state is often compared to turning on the lights in a dark room.

Pay attention to the sensations in your body. This is not to be confused with paying attention to what you think about your body or what you see when you look at your body. If you notice your intense emotions include rapid heart rate, shortness of breath, dizziness, rapid thoughts, tension, or other physical signals, this means that your body has invoked its powerful fight or flight response and you are emotionally hijacked. Your hijacked brain has primed your body for action. In order to cope with intense emotion, assuming you do not need to freeze, fight, or run for safety, you can do certain things to settle your brain and body. Just like rebooting a computer, there are ways to reboot your body. Slowing down your body clears the way for your brain to get unlocked from the intense emotion (what is going on inside of you) and focus on what is going on around you. Getting information about what is going on around us as well as inside of us positions us to develop a course of action, or at least our next helpful step.

The skills in this chapter can be used to physically reset your body when you find yourself emotionally hijacked. You can also find such skills in the resources section at the back of this book, where you will also find recommendations to find additional information and help.

Breathing To Settle Your Brain and Body

Bodies are made for shallow breathing or holding our breath when emotions are high. If someone says, "Take a deep breath," it seems to add to fear and frustration instead of help. They are trying to breathe but can only gasp for air and take in small amounts, which makes them hyperventilate and become more anxious. (Hyperventilation and anxiety have many symptoms in common.) If this happens to you, do three to four breaths where you tense your stomach muscles to push as much air as possible from the bottom of your stomach, then two additional puffs out. Next, relax your stomach totally and let the in breath naturally fill with air like a balloon. You will need to practice this way of deep breathing many times when you do not need it so you can use it when you need it.

 As soon as you can get air in, move to breathing in for four seconds and out for six seconds (paced breathing) or, breathe in for the count of four, hold your breath for the count of four, breathe out for the count of four, and hold for four (tactical or box breathing). You may need to adjust these numbers a little for your comfort so experiment; choose which works best for you and practice until you can do it automatically. You are overriding your body's survival instinct, thus extreme physical and emotional reactions, by breathing deeply and evenly when you are angry, afraid, or sad, and that does not happen easily. Making your breathing deeper, slower, and more regular is one of the most effective strategies for starting to reduce emotional arousal literally within one to two minutes.

Also, a daily deep or diaphragmatic breathing practice is beneficial in decreasing high emotion into the next day and will have a cumulative effect of decreased anxiety over time. Simply by taking regular, deep, full breaths throughout the day, you can improve your emotional, mental, and physical well-being and resilience.

When your body and emotions are hijacked, you can sit down right there, right then, regulate your breathing, and begin to settle your physical reactions and your emotions. You can take these breathing techniques anywhere you go! How cool is that? Now we're talking real control.

Other tools to help your body and brain settle are the Butterfly Hug (commonly used in Eye Movement Desensitization and Reprocessing (EMDR) therapy, Tapping/EFT (Emotional Freedom Techniques), and mindfulness of sensations in the body (Mindfulness Based Stress Reduction and DBT). Refer to the Resources section for more information. Mindful Self-Compassion (MSC) skills are also extremely useful as they combine the skills of mindfulness and self-compassion that demonstrate increased life satisfaction and decreased depression, anxiety, and stress. Get curious and learn more and more ways to help your brain and body settle when you are at the mercy of curveballs!

Being On Guard versus Being in Control

Eating Disorder Thought: "Since you can't handle hard things, always be on the lookout. Never let your guard down and cut pain off at the pass. That's how to stay in control."

Truth: If you don't swing, you may be less likely to strike out. You also will never get a base hit, much less a home run. The eating disorder has us think that intentionally "failing" will allow you to maintain some control. Actually, failing on your own terms gives you absolutely no control—and takes away your chances of having anything more. (I know, I know . . . at least you don't have far to fall when a risk doesn't work out.) Think about that. Exactly what is it that you have control over when you intentionally fail? Do you want to spend the rest of your life sitting in a grave to assure that you never fall into a hole and hurt yourself?

The part of you that is struggling with the eating disorder may believe that the eating disorder behaviors help you avoid fear, embarrassment, and pain. Shame and resilience researcher Brené Brown, PhD, LMSW calls this vulnerability, and with or without an eating disorder, vulnerability is unavoidable. If you swing at no pitches or throw down the bat and walk away, it might seem like you hold on to more dignity than if you swing and miss, strike out, and suffer embarrassment in front of everyone. Eating disorder thinking can lead you to believe that taking risks will result in a bigger fall than you can tolerate. Brown often discusses that her research has found that stating things you are grateful for can decrease the fear of being in vulnerability when we are afraid that good things will end or disaster will strike. She calls this "foreboding joy," and maintains that readying ourselves for tragedy to strike in the future actually squanders the joy we have in the moment.

Are you willing to consider a change from avoiding hard and scary things to learning how to identify them sooner and face them? Would you consider trying to muster some skills to help you stay in the game? It's difficult. If you practice and use the skills in this chapter over and over, you'll have your tools ready to use when necessary. If you stay with this strategy, bits of hope, confidence, and trust in yourself will begin to, almost imperceptibly, show up. You can't change the fact that a curveball has been thrown your way, but you can learn to see it for what it is and do something that will help address the problem instead of making matters worse.

So, okay. The curveball is in front of you. You have decided to respect that it is, indeed, a curveball—you hate it, you are shaking in your cleats, and you don't want any part of it. Ultimately you want this to go differently, because avoiding risks hasn't worked out so well. You use breathing to relax your body and willingly open your hands so you can decide what to do and what will be effective. You remind yourself that what you've got in the moment is what you've got for the moment. You use one of the previously listed skills, which brings the intensity of the emotion down some. You know your thoughts are good at tumbling around in your mind and causing more distress. Your job here is to add more skills and continue to use them, little by little, until your emotions seem to stabilize enough for you to think more clearly. What now?

Pause

Eating Disorder Thought: "There is no better way to get off of a spinning merry-go-round than to hang out with me."

Truth: It is true that getting lost in eating disorder thoughts and/or behaviors makes the chaos of things whirling around you disappear. The problem is that the merry-go-round hasn't actually stopped. You just closed your eyes. You are definitely not in charge.

Shift Gears

After you have reset your body you still may need to press pause and get your brain elsewhere while you let your feelings and your brain settle. My team of therapists who work with managing emotions developed the acronym DRIVEN to help remember tools that can be used to let the mind settle.

- **D**isengage: Step away, take a break, and get your distress down; Just do something else for awhile. Don't ruminate on the intense emotions or why you feel them. Create an imaginary or physical container and put thoughts and feelings in it. Take your mind to a calm, safe, or relaxing place.

- **R**eplace the Thoughts: Occupy your mind. Name an animal or city that begins with each letter of the alphabet; engage your mind with word, math, or logic puzzles; count backward from 100 by seven; play alphabet games; remember the birthdates of people in your life; count tiles on the floor; or count circles or squares in the room. Get your brain thinking. This helps bring the logical part of your brain back online to help decrease emotion.

- **I**nvolve yourself in other things: Throw yourself completely into another activity, and when your brain runs back to the painful emotion, bring it back to what you are now doing. Go to a movie; watch videos; do puzzles; knit; clean the house; go for a drive; play an instrument; play with a dog; call or visit a friend (talk about something other than the problem); play games. I like to go to a nearby dollar store and read greeting cards.
- **V**iewpoint: Change your view of the situation or the fact that you are in it.
- **E**motions: Do things that will create different, less distressing emotions. If you are sad, do things that make you laugh or feel peaceful; if you are angry, look at or listen to things that make you feel calm or peaceful or happy. Jiggle the emotion loose with activities that bring up a different feeling, like inspiring or funny videos or movies; upbeat, empowering, or calming music; funny, peaceful, or inspirational photos; or reading jokes or inspirational quotes. Burp (yes, I'm serious) or do something playful. Experiment with using various activities to learn what provokes different emotions for you.
- **N**eeds: Reach out to others in need or just be kind to others. Practice a random act of kindness; make something for someone; send cards, jokes, inspirational texts, or messages; babysit to give a parent a break; visit, entertain, or read to residents in a nursing home; visit someone who is lonely; run errands for someone in need.

Individualize these skills, experiment with them, and make them your own so they can help you. When you need them, stick with them, doing one after another, until you can think well enough to make real choices instead of doing the same old emotionally driven behaviors that bring you the same old results.

Spiritual practices like talking to a higher power or deity, reading or reciting scripted poems or prayers such as the Serenity Prayer or the Rosary, chanting, meditation, metta or loving kindness phrases, and many others can help decrease painful emotions.

Warning: Don't fall for the eating disorder's suggestions of going for a run or getting ice cream. Find activities that work for you but are not destructive, addictive, risky, or give eating disorder thoughts or behaviors any room to show up. Throw yourself completely into them. Your imagination is your only limitation. There is no need to box yourself in. Just make sure you don't use behaviors that suck you into checking out or shutting down to the degree that you avoid versus re-enter your life. Remember, the way to use skills to improve your ability to cope with curveballs in the long run is to pause, not shut down. That said, if you can find something to hold your attention that is legal, that is not harmful to others or yourself, go for it.

Wait, Wait, Wait . . .

At the amusement park near where I grew up, they wanted us to stay seated on rides until they stopped completely. The attendants would say, "Wait . . . wait . . . hold on . . . hold it . . . hold it . . . now get out!" It was their way of making sure everyone waited until it was safe to exit. To do otherwise presented unnecessary danger. So it is with emotions. As you are learning, in crisis times it takes a lot of holding on and a lot of "wait, wait, waits" to keep from prematurely unbuckling your seatbelt and jumping into trouble.

Use Your Senses

Robyn's mom soothed her when Robyn was sad or scared until, way too soon, her mom couldn't, and Robyn was sometimes left trying to soothe her pain by herself. Restricting nutrition, obsessing about calories, bingeing and purging, etc. all can provide the temporary function of soothing, but they are numbing and only reinforce that you cannot cope with pain without the eating disorder's help to numb it.

One of the most helpful ways to soothe yourself without causing additional harm is to immerse yourself in the present moment, using all of your senses instead of thoughts about what has or what will occur. Try putting your hand over your heart or on your shoulder or the back of your neck. You can look at photos of loved ones (not someone you have lost) and beautiful places; notice what you see on a walk; look at your pet, a loved one, a child, or flowers, and let what you see sink into your heart. Listen to music or other sounds that soothe you (make sure they actually soothe you). Touch a pet, a baby's hair, your own hair, a favorite or a weighted blanket; run your hand through a bowl of uncooked rice; use a heating pad; take a warm bath, using bubbles if you like the way they feel. Smell lotions, lavender, candles, coffee, hay, oils, or perfumes, but only those you really like. The sense of taste can be helpful for soothing, but due to the thoughts and emotions that can get wrapped up around food when an eating disorder is present, it's best just to leave your taste buds out of your toolkit for calming emotions.

Some people fall into soothing themselves more than they address the emotions in their lives, and it causes bigger problems later on. Many people think they don't deserve to be soothed or that others should soothe them. It is ultimately your job to soothe yourself when you need it, and help from others is a gift to be appreciated. What will work for you? Pay attention. Your body will tell you what it finds soothing.

 Look at the skills for tolerating intense and painful emotions in this chapter. Use my examples or create your own. Experiment with them. Play around with them. See which ones hold your attention. As you try one skill at a time, use the zero-to-one-hundred scale to rate the intensity of your emotion before and after. Even if you are not in crisis, you will still probably notice some decrease in negative mood and/or an increase in positive mood. See if you can choose four that seem helpful to use for yourself.

You may find yourself acting on eating disorder behaviors to help you tolerate distress. Remember, recovery is about turning your mind back to doing things differently and learning what you can about what went wrong before. It is like kicking dirt into the hole you keep falling into. With time, the hole will be less deep, causing less harm when you fall in and allowing you to get out sooner. As you practice pressing pause, preventing harmful reactions, and then responding to difficult situations, you build and start to trust the emotional strength and know-how that are needed to climb out of the trenches. You are better able to rely on your tools to cope rather than needing an eating disorder as your only choice.

I am me,
with all my emotions, flaws, beauty, and life lessons.
None of them define me.
Yet all of them make me.

Today, I will honor all that I am in its full integrity.
—*Robyn*

5.

Catch the Lies

Chinese Food and the Hot Malibu Sun

By Robyn

Giving up the behavior of the eating disorder was like the pain you feel after losing a lover. While I was ready to go through what I understood would be, initially, a painful process of ending my relationship with the illness, I held great fear of what my life would look like when I finally let go.

The disorder was my companion, my safety net, and my protection in a world where I felt too much. It kept me small, and that served me because sometimes I wanted to be small. I also wanted to feel beautiful to the world—to fit in with the western culture's beauty ideal. In recovery, I didn't know if that feeling was possible. I was scared. *Of course, I was.* By questioning why I would miss the eating disorder, I was acknowledging my role in keeping it.

I had become so attached to the eating disorder that it was a part of my identity. Like any unhealthy relationship, when two become one, it creates a dependency where we may begin to question whether life can even continue without that relationship. I was enmeshed with the eating disorder, and I was the one who had to start detangling myself from it.

I had long since noticed the lies of the disorder. I saw them, and I chose to ignore them. If I wanted recovery though, I'd have to identify the lies and also my part within the unhealthy relationship. Owning our part within the illness is probably one of the hardest things any of us do in the recovery process. When recovering from any mental illness, a great deal of compassion and patience with ourselves, and anyone else experiencing one, is essential to the recovery process. Sometimes that's hard to do, right? I get it.

Owning our part within the illness is probably one of the hardest things any of us do in the recovery process.

I use to think my part was just about exposing the illness. As if it were like going to get your purse and catching someone you love with their hand in it. You know there is something amiss, but you don't say anything. Now, I believe that my part is more about being willing to no longer steal from the same purse that the eating disorder steals from. I do this by no longer acting out self-destructive behaviors.

I believed that others judged me by my size because I once judged myself and others by their size. I compared myself to others all the time, and found strength in being thinner and shame in being larger. I starved at people and ate at myself—a brutal punishment either way. Just because I wanted to end the eating disorder didn't mean that I wanted to feel big and unattractive. I had and still have a desire to feel my best, to feel good in my skin, but the eating disorder behavior was doing the opposite. My body was dying. Somehow, I had to begin to trust others and have faith that there was more to me, and indeed to my life, than my body—despite all the images that flashed on the TV, magazines, and screens that told me otherwise. But most importantly, I knew if I wanted to be rid of the eating disorder, I had to be willing to reevaluate my need to control the world through my body and define myself through the images of a broken body-image culture.

◆ ◆ ◆

At nineteen I had my first relationship with an English man named Dylan. Dylan was the first guy who had shown interest in me. He was good looking, and being in a relationship advertised to those around me that I could be loved, even though I didn't feel lovable.

Dylan slapped me across the face within weeks of our first make-out session. It was about 8 p.m. and we were lying in his room, fully clothed on a mattress that lay on the floor. He said something, I don't know what. I straddled him teasingly, and then he slapped me. I held the left side of my face, shocked. But instead of leaving Dylan immediately, I rode my bicycle in the dark to buy Chinese food for him. I apologized for his behavior, just as I apologized for so many wasted years for the disorder's behavior. It was the only way I could make it right in my mind to stay with him. I protected his behavior and justified it by creating a story that would keep me with him because, despite the abuse, he told me that I had a chance of love. Just like the eating disorder, the price of having such "love" was high, but I thought I needed it.

One evening, a few months into our relationship, I sat on the foyer steps inside a movie theatre. Dylan sat beside me, telling me how fat I was. We had just had an argument, and he knew that I believed I needed him more than he needed me. He sat there telling me how his last girlfriend was a personal trainer and so much better looking than me. Again, I didn't leave him. Instead, I perceived it as the need to try harder. It was during that argument I learned what I thought to be the value of starving. Starving, I told myself, would make Dylan want me. I played small so I would not to feel too much. Recovery demands that I begin to own me—all of me. Honor me. And by doing this, I begin to teach people how to treat me.

◆ ◆ ◆

One Sunday evening when I was sixteen, I opened the garage door and walked into the smoky, dark, garage designed as a "man cave" for my father. It was a place he practically lived in. The garage was quiet with only the sound of Dad inhaling and exhaling his cigarette. I was wearing my mother's pink satin pajamas that made me feel comforted and slimmer, as they draped baggily on my frame.

Dad was sitting, staring at the wall, glancing every now and then at the one thing he gave himself—a six-by-six-inch TV that was bolted to the same brick wall. He was bare-chested and his stomach rolled over his blue shorts that rode up to gather at the top of his thighs.

Dad loved to hear me read my poetry, and I loved feeling pride when I heard his response to me performing it. As I stood beside him, the smoke rising up from the ashtray burned my eyes, but nothing would stop me sharing my poem with him. I gave voice to my poem, which shared of my frustration and deep desire to leave my body, so I could be free. It was a beautifully dark poem, full of insight for a sixteen-year-old.

I finished the poem and just stood there.

I waited for his approval, his identification. I waited for us to bond.

As he took a puff from his cigarette, he looked down to the cold, concrete floor, then straight into my eyes with conviction and compassion. Doing his very best to protect me from more pain he said, "That's great, Robbie. But don't share that with anyone. They could use it against you."

Confused, I said, "Okay, Dad," and left the garage with a new sense of *I am too much. I am not enough.* The smoke didn't bother me anymore.

Many years later, after I was completely free of eating disorder behaviors, I learned to embody myself more. I was having a conversation with my husband and our close friend, Michael. Michael was a TV star in Hollywood, and he was one of the funniest people—besides my husband—I had ever met. But there was another side of Michael; behind all that celebrity business, he was vulnerable. His self-deprecating humor gave his friends glimpses into his challenging childhood and mental state. Hanging out with Michael made me understand that people should not be judged by what they have achieved, but rather by who they are as human beings. No one is ever protected from the pain of life, no matter what you have or how you look.

One morning, drinking coffee in the Malibu sun, I had a conversation with Michael and Tim. It was a conversation that allowed me to finally confront the lie that my size was what earned me love and respect. During that time in Malibu, I was thinner than I am now and still maintaining the belief that how I looked was the basis of how much people liked me. I admit, it's a hard belief to be rid of. Our culture supports and promotes such belief. If it didn't, there'd be nothing to buy to make us believe we are doing better.

During coffee that morning, I was arguing that if I were ten pounds heavier, those I loved would not be as fond of me. They not only balked at that statement, they were genuinely horrified by it. That got my attention. I heard them, and I also heard that my belief hurt them and discounted their character and integrity. "We love you because of you. If you were a supermodel and you were an a*hole of a person, we wouldn't like you."

And that is the truth. Nothing more. Nothing less.

Really, eating disorders, although they feel like it, are not about the food and the size of our thighs, waist, wrists, or any other part of the body we have overly focused on changing. And the problem is not about the eating disorder or the Dylans or the alcohol or any other substance we choose to use to numb the world out with and calm our minds from. It's about our relationship to them. If it were truly about those things, if they were the actual problem, wouldn't the entire world population have a problem with them too?

It's not that we are incapable of getting out of the unhealthy relationship with [fill in the blank]. It's the power we have given [fill in the blank] so that when faced with a choice between the unfamiliar and the familiar, we choose the familiar no matter how painful. We choose the unhealthy relationship. I kept going back to the eating disorder because it had its benefits. And I knew exactly what I was going to get. There is a sense of comfort in the familiar. That was my part.

Let the Sun Illuminate the Lies

By Espra

Dieting Will Make You Thin. Umm . . . False!
Eating Disorder Thought: "If you just use enough willpower, you can lose the weight, reach your goal, and your life will finally be good."
Truth: Dieting will make you *hungry*. Dieting will make you *gain weight*. Research shows us that diets eventually fail and those individuals gain back even more weight than they lost.

Breathing is a basic biological need. Holding your breath deprives your body of oxygen, which is necessary for survival. If it is not getting enough oxygen, your body will take over and breathe for you. Your force of will cannot control this forever. Taking a big gulp of air is not a failure of willpower. Sooner or later, it is destined to happen.

Eating is a basic biological need. Dieting deprives your body of food and nourishment, which are necessary for survival. Dieting causes physical (and psychological) deprivation and hunger. If it is not getting enough nutrition, your body will take over and eat for you. Sooner or later it is destined to happen, and you will likely binge or eat in an out of control way. Your force of will cannot control this forever. "Breaking" a diet by eating or bingeing is not a failure of willpower.

Surely, you know someone (maybe yourself) who has gone on a diet, gone off, and resumed it (or another diet) later. How many diets can you recall that have come and gone over the years? Think about it this way: If these diets made people lose weight and keep it off, why would new ones need to be dreamed up? The more diets fail, the more money people spend on diets. The diet industry gets rich while individuals get miserable and develop eating disorders.

More and more evidence is emerging that dieting causes binge eating and weight gain. Restricting calories or consistently spending more calories than you take in causes your metabolism to decrease, causing your body to store fat. Weight loss stops because your brilliant body holds on to precious calories needed for survival.

Some people are now catching on that diets don't work so the diet industry is adjusting by disguising diets as "lifestyle changes." Let's face it, if it involves restricting amounts and/or limiting food types, imposing rules on what you can and cannot eat—it's a diet. Dieting results in repeated weight loss followed by weight gain. There is evidence that this "yo-yo" effect is extremely hard on bodies and health.

And speaking of dieting, here's a sneaky eating disorder trick: Have you ever noticed that when you're dieting, the eating disorder moves the bar on weight loss? Maybe you recognize thoughts like, *Just a little lower will be even better*, or *A little more off the thighs will get you into those quadruple zero jeans*, or *Lose just a little more and you'll feel confident enough to talk to people at parties.* Come on. See it. Catch the lies. Watch the bar moving. How long does the eating disorder stay happy with any accomplishment before it wants more from you?

Why Do You Really Want to Lose Weight?

Eating Disorder Thought: "Skinny people get more respect, opportunities, and relationship options in our society. You can't deny that fat people are treated differently from skinny people."

Truth: I can promise you there are many ways to meet your goals beyond forcing your body into a mold. I believe it because I have walked beside countless individuals who have discovered ways to meet their goals independently of their body's shape and size.

Watch out: Believing that your body must be a certain way to accomplish the things that people of different shapes and sizes have accomplished is thinking you're an exception to the rule.

To be fair, there seems to be some evidence to back up, some of the time, some of the "benefits" of eating disorders that clients have taught me over the years. But you must consider the short-term benefits versus the long-term benefits. Is it worth dying just so you can talk to people at parties or get the job you seek? Is it worth dying just to keep your partner from looking at someone else? Are you absolutely certain that if your body looked the way you want it to, the things you desire would be firmly in your hands? Are you 100 percent certain there are no other variables?

You and the eating disorder are not one. You have different hopes, dreams, long-term goals, and paths to tread. Even if you believe you are one with the eating disorder because it can accomplish these things for you, it is not true. You can accomplish goals and have a life of your desire without it. Very few people start out with the intent to develop an eating disorder. It merely joins you somewhere along the path.

I hope you can pinpoint what drives the eating disorder. Okay, I get it; obviously I must not know much about eating disorders because the point is to get skinny, right? But maybe there's something more to the story. Eating disorders and/or their symptoms can provide or appear to provide many benefits.

Consider the following as just a few of the reasons why people use eating disorder behaviors and see whether some of them apply to you. As always, don't try to force them to apply if they don't.

- To be accepted
- To feel worthwhile or loveable
- To prove you are not worthwhile or loveable
- To be different, unique, or special
- For protection
- To be admired or to be good at something
- For self-punishment
- To be nurtured
- To help others see your emotional pain or suffering

Here are just a few of the bottom-line emotions that drive eating disorders and/or related behaviors: self-disgust, shame, worthless, unlovable, invisible, alienated, flawed, or bad (due to some reason that you may or may not be able to put your finger on).

In terms of relationships, the eating disorder may convince you that it will help you find a relationship or make your relationships better by making you feel more confident and outgoing or more accepted by others. There may be the hope that the eating disorder will bring distance, protection, decreased expectations, or the chance to avoid intimacy.

 What does the eating disorder convince you is obtainable by using eating disorder behaviors, losing weight, having the perfect body, or even having the disorder itself? Does it tell you that these things will be harder or impossible to accomplish without your eating disorder? Write down your thoughts about this.

The eating disorder may be driven by severe judgment and insults heaped on you by peers, siblings, other family members, or dating partners. Others in your life may criticize your body and reinforce your feelings of worthlessness. Dating partners are often the perpetrators of this verbal, physical, and sexual abuse. So often, it is a secret that is hidden by shame because the battering words are believed to be true. Increased efforts to "do better" at eating disorder behaviors often feel like the only hope for being loved and accepted. "Who do I need to be for you to accept me?" you may ask. Like Robyn, you will find that being skinny is not the route to self-esteem and love.

The Real Payoffs of an Eating Disorder

Eating Disorder Thought: "Don't fall for this one. You've seen the outcome; there's no way to deny it, because it's a *fact*. Others notice and want to be around thin people. Take that, you know-it-alls!"

Truth: Your eating disorder does not allow you to see beyond a short-term and immediate goal. Your longer-term goals (with which you may be out of touch or not even know) are ignored and not considered. For example, lying and deception (which may violate your long-term values) are constant companions of eating disorders. Ongoing behavior that conflicts with your values increases shame, erases self-respect, and erodes relationships.

Eating disorders develop lives of their own by overtaking the thoughts, emotions, behaviors, spirits, and identities of those they inhabit. The eating disorder can tell you that it will ensure you have what you perceive as special and highly desirable relationships with others. But when acting out of your

Eating disorders develop lives of their own by overtaking the thoughts, emotions, behaviors, spirits, and identities of those they inhabit.

eating disorder, these relationships tend to get superficial and conditional, based on appearance, and continued out of obligation. Conflict, tension, or withdrawal by loved ones is typical, and interaction becomes about the food or eating disorder behaviors. Social and dating relationships lack depth and emotional intimacy due to preoccupation with food, your body, eating, exercising, purging, and withdrawal to engage in eating disorder behaviors.

The eating disorder fails to respect others as individuals as well. Although it is true that some people can't see beyond cheeks, thighs, and pounds, other people can. Please give people the chance to speak for themselves about what they value and like. Please give other people the respect of believing them (or at least pretending you do) when they tell you the truth about how they see you. Everyone does not see you as an object that is only a size or weight. Please do not insult me by telling me that therapists are supposed to see things this way. As I tell my clients, therapist wages don't pay me enough to be a liar.

Write down a short list of your values. Put an "x" by any that you regularly violate because of the eating disorder. The eating disorder will only take you so far if you are living out of sync with your core values, and you will not have the self-respect that comes from aligning with your values. Keep this list and read it regularly to help you talk back to the eating disorder.

Keep looking at the eating disorder thoughts. Consider that you and the eating disorder do not have to be one and the same. Since you are not an exception to the rest of the human race (and if you believe that people have an essence that is essentially good) then consider, too, that you might also have an authentic identity outside of your disorder.

With education, help, hope, and perseverance, you can sift through the rubble to gather and mold together pieces of the worthwhile, lovable, and true identity that is uniquely yours.

Fight the good fight.
Go against the grain.
Question your eating disorder.
Do something even when it feels too difficult.
Live.

Today, check in with yourself and question anything you feel adamant about; it could be the eating disorder. Ask yourself: Does the thought you are having serve you in your new quest for recovery and self-worth? Be honest about it. If you find that the belief speaks against your well-being, throw it out. If it is one of self-worth, keep it, and know that you have just taken one more step toward victory.

—Robyn

6.

From the Life Raft to the Shore

Northern Shore Beauty and Casted Spells of Ugliness

By Robyn

North Sydney is a place where art and corporations mix, creating an alluring cocktail of possibilities. Settled within layers of deep history, mirrored in the old Sydney town of residential homes and ocean shores, then sprinkled with the newness of high-rises and hip establishments, the Northern Shores represented old money and new elegance. It was a place I loved to be. Walking its affluent streets always brought with it a sense of giddiness. It also bought with it great anxiety. My feeling of unworthiness went everywhere with me, including all the places that brought me joy.

I was drawn to North Sydney in my late teens. My parents had agreed to send me to a private performing arts school in Sydney, and they had decided to move us from the central coast into the suburbs of Sydney to prevent the two-hour-each-way train commute that we all endured daily until the move. The performing arts school was filled with talented wannabes who mostly came from wealthy homes. I was not one of them (from a wealthy home that is), but I pretended to be. My mother managed to get me a bursary (a partial scholarship) for the school. She was as committed to supporting my dreams as I was to following them.

One late morning, just before the lunch school bell rang, Melinda Williams walked into the school like she owned it. Tall, with a gymnast's physique and stunning crystal-blue eyes, Melinda was a rising childhood star. She had what we all wanted—a career already started in the film industry. Her own sense of importance made me want to be her best friend immediately. Everything about her spelled fabulous including her laughter (ladylike) and her presence (captivating).

Melinda came from a newly broken home and lived with her father and stepmother in the suburbs of North Sydney—McMahons Point. I had passed this train stop with my mother plenty of times while traveling to and from her workplace or her lupus specialist, where I would sit in the waiting room, uneasily waiting to have her blood count results revealed. Each month, they'd bring with them either a sense of being able to breathe again or a sense of doom. But now Melinda was going to open my eyes and show me not only North Sydney, but the life that I had been waiting for, the life of an actor— glamour, spritzes (half wine, half soda water), and all the gifts that money can afford felt present in the heart of North Sydney, and indeed, McMahons Point.

No one tells you that eating disorders are *hopeless*. When I was enmeshed in the eating disorder, I felt the opposite. I believed it would keep me safe and in control, and make me desirable. I thought it was there to protect me from *myself*. I felt applauded and admired for my overly thin body, and snidely giggled at when I was larger. I defined myself based on how I believed I was being judged by the women around me. I walked those streets of North Sydney as both a binge eater and a restrictor. I felt approved of when I was thin and wanted to hide or apologize for myself when I was larger than I wanted to be. However, I always felt larger than I wanted to be, even at my thinnest. This was one of the abusive ways the thought processes of eating disorder kept me in check, like a school bully with their fist.

I experienced a sense of coolness when I was thin—but without *any* sense of self. Somehow, restricting gave me a feeling of belonging and an illusion of control that made me feel acceptable. This feeling of acceptability was stamped into my psyche, as was the sense memory that measured my happiness. The problem was that it was rare and unpredictable. Underneath laid no foundation and no understanding of how to find and measure my sense of self. I couldn't self-soothe as I aimlessly followed the directions of the eating disorder. My body image was so entwined with my passion to be a working actor that the failure of not fitting the model of "thin, stunning, and flawless" dictated my life. I 100 percent believed I needed the eating disorder to keep me in line; it was my measuring stick for success.

Dylan's abuse, too, made it easier for me to buy into such distorted beliefs. It was all so compelling and affirmed the need for me to strive for thinness— for perfection—whatever that is. I used Dylan's abuse and aligned it with the eating disorder's, a double whammy of protection against myself. It was a painful existence.

I joined my first acting agency, also in North Sydney, at the age of sixteen. It was tucked behind a high-end shopping mall in the heart of everything that was happening. When I first was preparing to meet my agent, I had been vigorously dieting and was hopeful that my body would elicit approval, praise even. It was not uncommon for an agent's assistant to comment on my weight. She once told me that I could afford to lose some pounds. She sat on her white, abundantly padded leather chair behind her desk covered in black and white headshots, faxes, and audition scripts, and compared me to one of my childhood friends who was also on the agency's roster. With my broken glasses, I perceived my friends as far prettier than me. They were stunning with model-like attributes. I felt like an ugly duckling beside them.

During the start of my career, I also had a photographer telling me how horrible my smile was when taking my headshots. "You mustn't smile," he said. "You'll ruin my photos!" I laughed at his antics but came away with a new rule for myself. I took both the assistant's and photographer's statements as gospel and allowed these memories of being put in my place to remind me of how little chance I had of succeeding—*See! I need the eating disorder behavior to help me become the person* they *want me to be.*

Later, Dylan and I lived on the Northern Shores battling within our dysfunctional relationship and damaging our future together. And yet, so many wonderful things happened in North Sydney too. I created strong friendships and memories that still bring me tremendous joy just thinking about them. Life is made up of both pain and joy; I understand that now. I got my first big break as an actor when I lived there, acting alongside the likes of Sam Neil, Greta Scacchi, and an amazing, established Australian cast that I felt both blessed and overwhelmed to be in the presence of. I went to my first movie premiere, too. I watched myself up on the cinema screen with my mother by my side. (My mother praised; I criticized.) After the premiere and press photos, we tipsily walked home through the streets of McMahons Point with no shoes on; our feet ached from the newly purchased heels we both wore for the special celebration. My mum's feet, eroded by the side effects of lupus, had no padding to soften the impact from bone to road. Still, she giggled, grateful for the lubrication of the champagne we had shared. Nothing would get in the way of celebrating her youngest daughter's success. I had my twenty-first birthday celebration on the North Shore as well. I discovered life in all its fullness there. I had my first panic attack there, my first ride in an ambulance, and my first real heartbreak, too.

When I finally got the courage (fueled by panic attacks) to cut off my relationship with Dylan, the eating disorder began to take on other forms. Anxiety gripped me daily. I always felt like I was waiting for something horrible to happen or at any moment I would topple over the cliff of crazy never to return. I thought every feeling I had was real and that if I just stopped for even a moment, the feelings would engulf me. Taking refuge at my parents' home in Belfield, I clung onto my Dad's back as he piggy-backed me around the living room, both of us screaming: "Fuck off, panic attacks! You will not get me." Both my Dad and I were petrified of who I had become at twenty-two years old and feared for my sanity. Too thin, malnourished, and unable to fight off the consequences of continually performing the eating disorder behavior, I began to suffer even more severe panic attacks. All the years of trying to be in control—of myself, of my mum's health, and of my own destiny—left me feeling emotionally robbed. I wish I could say that the end of the eating disorder was near. But it was not. It took me another seven years to have the courage to end that relationship too.

I am a sensitive soul. I see who I was as a child when I look into the eyes of my own daughters, Lilly and Chloe. Lilly's creativity and passion to be heard, along with her deep empathy for others, make me brace myself at times. I take comfort in knowing that I am healthy and aware of my children's temperament traits—a combination of mine, Tim's, and some they came into the world with. My daughters will have their own stories that I cannot control, just as I could not control my mum's disease. But I continue to be here for them— healthy, present, and accepting—just the way my Mum was there for me.

One day when getting out of the car after picking both girls up from school, I asked Lilly where her brand-new poncho was. "I don't know! I don't know!" she wailed, as if I had asked her where her little sister was after losing her. The panic began to rise in her, and she ran from me as if I were a monster. Trying to be neutral and not caught up in my own fear that her panic triggers in me, I asked her to come back to me. In an attempt to honor her feelings but to also encourage her to take in her surroundings, as they were in reality, I put my arm around her shoulders and asked her to look into my eyes so she could be sure to see my truth. "Lilly, can you see that Mommy is not angry? I just asked you where your poncho was. Can you see that this is all that is going on?" She nodded with tears in her eyes.

Her emotions had already begun to consume her, like mine used to—who am I kidding?—still can. But now I know better, and because of it, I get to help her as a parent. I can teach her, both of my girls when needed, to self-soothe, something my parents didn't know how to do. My mum was always there to console me, but I never learned how to console myself. As I went on to tell Lilly that there was nothing else happening that brought about the need for fear, she began to understand and come to. We talked about where she'd last left the poncho, and whether it was in her classroom cubby.

"But what if I can't find the poncho, Mom?" She began to panic again.

"Then we will learn that when we take things off at school, we need to put them in your cubby so you know where they are. But right now, you believe it is in your classroom, correct?" "Yes," she nodded.

"So tomorrow we will pick it up. It is not a big deal. Okay?"

"Okay." She smiled. The following day we retrieved the poncho from where she had left it, in her classroom cubby.

◆ ◆ ◆

I continued to lose endless days in my mid-to-late-twenties as I intensely focused on concocting ways to either stay thin or lose weight. With no boyfriend adding to the fuel of my need to be something for him, I had lost the ability to *stay* thin for long periods of time, so most of my time was now spent on trying to get back there. My weight fluctuation wreaked havoc on my acting career—or so I convinced myself. And at the same time, I was also quietly beginning to say no to the eating disorder. I slowly established some form of truth outside of the tiny world and all-consuming relationship I once lived in. The disorder was still there, and had a presence of authority, but its spell was beginning to wear off. I just didn't know how to break it completely. I had moments where I questioned what my relationship with it served, and with that came moments of awareness that it was I who allowed the eating disorder take me down—and coupled with my anxiety, it would take my life if I let it.

One wintry afternoon in 1999, while working in a corporate office as a temp, I got a long-awaited call from my agent. I lived for those calls. There was an audition that day in North Sydney for a telephone commercial. Immediately I checked in with my body, and the eating disorder shut me down. *You look fat and unsophisticated. Say no to the audition and don't waste your time. You won't get it anyway.* I had been growing sick and tired of being knocked down by the negative blows of the eating disorder. I had begun to recognize what was happening in my relationship with it, just like I had toward the end of my abusive relationship with Dylan. I knew that just because both of them provided a ton of noise when I went against their directions, I still had the choice to change things and say no. That day, as I sat at the reception desk filtering calls for a bunch of fun-loving, cocaine dabbling, and money-hungry traders, I began to question the narrative I was telling myself:

Is it true that the casting agency wants only wafer-thin perfect-looking girls for the role they are casting? No.

Is it true that they will immediately judge me for what I look like and not for how I act? No.

Is it true that I don't deserve to participate in acting because of my current body size? NO.

The well-oiled thought process of the eating disorder automatically fired, but with every negative, eating disordered thought, I questioned, short-circuiting the eating disorder behavior response. I had become willing to wait and let the facts reveal themselves instead of beating myself up with the old, negative beliefs that kept me trapped in the eating disorder relationship. I decided to go to the audition anyway. Even if it was just for the duration of the audition, I promised myself to own my ability to act and not allow the eating disorder to come into the audition room with me. It could stay in the waiting room with all the other gorgeous young ladies, comparing my thighs with theirs. I walked into the audition room alone, unapologetic, and was hired later that day.

To this day, questioning the truth and the stories I tell myself is a source of empowerment. When I am tired or stressed, I still need to be conscious of not taking my negative thoughts so seriously. After all, just because I think it doesn't make it real. I see this same sense of empowerment come naturally to my daughter Chloe, even though she too is wonderfully sensitive. You can be sensitive and strong. Instinctively, Chloe often pauses without a word and observes the world around her. Sometimes, when I tell her she can't do something, she will begin to whine, then stop and say, "But why, Mommy?"

One day at our little town fair, I put both Lilly and Chloe on a kids' ride that spun around. Lilly was thrilled as the ride began to twirl slowly, though quite quickly for a toddler. In a rare moment, Lilly lifted her hands with pure excitement and reckless abandon, while Chloe looked over to me with a look in her eyes that said, "How the hell did I get here, and who are you people?" I laughed with a joy that will forever remain with me. She is our teacher, and we are hers, providing lessons of balance, creativity, the unforgiving power of fear, and the true sense of self that combats it. What a beautiful life. God is good.

The Beauty and the Beast Within

By Espra

Emotions 101

Eating Disorder Thought: "Skip this section. You know everything you need to know about emotions. Get rid of the bad ones as fast as you can."

Truth: A lack of understanding about emotions and how they work is an obstacle to recovery as much as it is an obstacle to healthy, resilient living. Learning how emotions operate and how to navigate them will give you an edge in managing your feelings, thoughts, urges, and behaviors, without needing an eating disorder to do so for you. This is the path to creating a life that has more peace, meaning, and value as it begins to align with your authentic values and goals.

One of the most important things to understand about emotions is that they begin in our brain and then the brain gets the entire body in on the action. Every emotion is created in hardwired circuits deep in our brain. These circuits activate neurochemicals, which cause physical reactions to incoming information often before we even know what is happening. When your brain detects incoming information from your environment, or even your thoughts, it automatically searches its existing database for your experiences and beliefs about yourself, others, and the world. I refer to this as "stories in our head" from Brené Brown's shame resilience work. Each set of physical changes has been fine-tuned over thousands of years to get your body to do what it determines is needed for you to have the best chance of survival and well-being. These body sensations and changes are what we call emotions.

Emotions are so body-based that we naturally refer to them in terms of the related physical reactions: "I just wanted to crawl into a hole," or "I was frozen with fear," or "I wanted to strangle them." The brain decides which chemicals and impulses to send through the body to get the body to either slow down or deliver additional energy. Emotional responses are instant and instinctive, and the brain's ability to put our bodies into action works at a speed that can be compared to traveling 200 to 300 miles per hour.

As an emotion surges through the body, creating its unique pattern of physical effects, it hijacks our attention and takes our thoughts, urges, and often our behavior with it. The emotion dictates our thoughts and then our thoughts fuel the emotion to keep it going. This is what's happening when we say something like, "I was so angry I couldn't think straight." We are not in our thinking mind. Our brains begin to collect thoughts that increase the emotion. For example, feeling scared or anxious causes us to think about past or possible future things that make us more anxious. Our survival has relied on emotions and thoughts fueling each other. If a bear were chasing you, your survival would depend on your thoughts reminding you of how afraid you are. The thoughts would give your body more energy to run, fight, or hide.

There are other times when our brains register information that leads to emotions that set off a chain of thoughts and behaviors that is harmful instead of helpful. For example, if you are scared that you will be judged or rejected if others see your body or see you eating, your brain plugs the information into a threat database, like with the bear. Then your body might instinctively try to avoid, run away, and hide. That response of isolation or withdrawal would be harmful instead of helpful in moving toward most values and goals, but it is automatic.

Since emotions are biological responses that affect the entire body, trying to push away painful emotions is like trying to push or slow down water in a river. It takes a lot of effort for no real results. You need a new approach to emotions to stabilize the chaos you might experience in their wake. Instead of trying to change the course of your emotions, consider learning how to ride the constant current of your emotions to work in your favor, in the way they were created to work. Emotions are messengers that can bring information to us (and others) about what is going on around us and ways we can respond. If we know how to use them, emotions give us an advantage and help us respond to life in an informed and meaningful way.

What I'm talking about is being mindful, aware, and paying attention to the signals as information and carefully observing your sensations, emotions, thoughts, urges, and behaviors. This is called mindfulness, and I have heard

Jon Kabat-Zinn, mindfulness master and teacher say, "Mindfulness means being awake. It means knowing what you are doing." Marsha Linehan, PhD, the developer of DBT, describes that being mindful is like turning on the lights to walk across a room full of furniture instead of walking across the room in the dark. When did the first signals start? Is your brain reacting to the person or situation or to your thoughts about that person or situation (the stories in your head)? Name these things. Only after clearly identifying and allowing all of the information into your awareness can you be aware enough to decide how to deliberately respond and what step to take first or next rather than react. Many who have used eating disorder behaviors to cope with emotions find that they can begin to see a first, best step, which is different than eating, restricting, or getting rid of calories in an attempt to cope with emotion.

Jon Kabat-Zinn created a simple, quick, and profoundly powerful mindfulness tool named STOP to help us slow down our reactions in the attempt to respond versus react to or numb what is actually going on.

S – Stop. Push pause. Say nothing. Do nothing. Totally stop everything for a moment.

T – Take deep breaths. Start with about four or five deep breaths.

O – Observe what you can see, hear, touch—your physical sensations and your thoughts about the situation.

P – Proceed mindfully. Make a plan about how you will proceed mindfully then put it into action.

Experiment with using STOP instead of using eating disorder thoughts and behaviors to guide you in responding to life events. It takes work and practice to replace the stories in your head with this simple tool. From this place you can respond to information and life with more wisdom, awareness, intention, and power than when your chemistry and body dictate your thinking and behavior. This is authentic power, and authentic power is a building block of recovery.

Allowing emotions to work in their natural way helps to keep them from getting stuck or dammed up and gives us protection against "drowning in emotion." Working with our emotions helps decrease the unnecessary suffering they can cause by hijacking our ability to think clearly, then dragging our behaviors along with them. Working with, instead of against, emotions is essential if you want full recovery that heals not only eating disorder behaviors, but also eating disorder urges and thoughts. It will heal your life.

Over time, working with the inherent way that emotions flow increases your ability to respond deliberately to life in the most effective ways possible and contributes to a life that feels worth living. It might mean that you talk with someone you trust, journal, scratch out the parts that are stories in your head and leave only the facts, allow emotions to flow through your body using a mindfulness exercise. I recommend the free "Working With Difficult Emotions" download on Christopher Germer's website, chrisgermer.com, or "Soften, Soothe, Allow: Working With Emotions in the Body" on Kristin Neff's website, self-compassion.org. Each of these practices takes only about fifteen to twenty minutes (much less time than engaging in eating disorder behaviors or preoccupation). You can work to change the hard emotions to different ones by (no, not using the eating disorder), deliberately applying actions like choosing music, short videos, photos, serving others, or other things to create less painful emotions, like peaceful, powerful, or happy ones.

Know What's Eating You
Eating Disorder Thought: "No brainer. Being *fat* is what's eating you."
Truth: Early in treatment when I ask my clients how they feel, they will usually reply, "I feel fat." You may feel fat, but notice how you feel "fatter" when you feel hard emotions and maybe not quite as miserably fat when you are in less emotional pain.

People can identify an average of five emotions. Try it now. See how many you can name. Once you learn how to label emotions, how they function, and how they are expressed verbally and nonverbally, you can see them at work across species. (I know when my dog experiences happiness, love, disgust, anger, and shame because he shows the same posture and gestures that humans show with similar emotions.) People tend to cope better with hard emotions after learning more about their nature. I have heard mindfulness researcher, Daniel Siegel, MD, professor of psychiatry at the UCLA School of Medicine and director of the Mindsight Institute, say that we can decrease the intensity of a painful emotion by up to seventy percent if we just label it and give it a name.

Looking at emotions in their most basic form can help decrease your hard feelings about having hard feelings as it minimizes the stories in our head about emotions. Stories in our head over careful observation tend to increase painful emotion. My clients often find it helpful to look at the benefits of emotions through the example of being a member of a tribe with the need to protect and help one another survive: You head to a field of planted crops and see another tribe taking the food that you planted to help your tribe survive the winter. Your eyes quickly take in this situation, and you immediately conclude that the food you need for survival is about to be lost. Your body instantly creates physical and mental energy as a resource and sends chemicals, signals, and impulses that prepare your body to fight or chase away the grazers in order to keep your food. We call this anger, and in this example anger would increase your chance of survival.

The emotion of fear helps us avoid danger as it either energizes or shuts down the body to get the threat away from us (fight), get us away from the threat (flee), or hide (freeze). The brain searches its database, quickly determines which fear response to create in our bodies, and makes it happen. Sometimes the automatic reaction urges us to do what is most effective under the circumstances, and other times it does not. When we are afraid or anxious, our breathing gets shallow and quick, muscles tense, and the heart races. Once fear is surging chemically through the body and the brain, it brings our thoughts along, using them as fuel to continue to propel the emotion. However, if fear is driving your body to run away when you need to interact in a scary social situation, it will not help you survive, and it will get in your way. With fear, sometimes if you need to act, you cannot; and sometimes if you need to mellow out, you cannot. It is hardly possible to engage in action that is logical because the body and the brain dictate both current thinking and continue to bring thoughts along for the ride.

The emotion of sadness pulls our attention inward while we regroup after a loss or disappointment. Ideally it lets others know that we need support, protection, and closeness. When sadness flows through us unobstructed, it helps us gather time and support as we grieve and gather our reserves to resume our lives in a changed way. When sadness cannot flow through us naturally, it can lead to long-term withdrawal, avoidance, and depression.

Embarrassment and guilt act like glue for relationships as they help us refrain from doing things that compromise our relationships with others and ourselves. These emotions get us to mend any damage we have done in relationships. For example, embarrassment and guilt can keep us from lying or stealing, or help us repair the damage to ourselves and others when we do. However, when guilt persists after we have mended the harm we caused, it can become destructive. Guilt and embarrassment (or shame) can become like playground bullies that jump out at us, beat us up, and knock us down over and over, just because they can. In this way, misplaced guilt and shame can take our freedom and drain our spirit. If you consistently feel guilt because of what, when, or how much you have eaten, this guilt can take over your thoughts, your behaviors, and your life. Robyn exposes the risks of misplaced shame when she talks about feeling approved of when she was thin and wanting to hide or apologize when her body was larger than she wanted it to be. This is an example of how eating disorder behaviors like binging, restricting, or purging seem to relieve guilt and shame. The instant relief encourages the behaviors to be repeated. The emotions feel like the beast within, and the eating disorder that seems to tame the beast can kill you.

Jealousy and envy give us energy so we can improve ourselves, our environment, and hold on to what's important to us. The emotion of envy is evident when young siblings propel their development forward as they compete to outdo one another. But sometimes these emotions can lead to behaviors that alienate others and get in the way of improving ourselves or our environment. If envy or jealousy motivates you to strive at any cost to be "skinnier," "restrict better," get rid of ingested calories to fit an ideal, be good enough, or be better than others, it can destroy your relationships, your health, and it can take your life.

In order to survive we must avoid things that can physically, emotionally, or mentally harm us. When we say another's actions "turn my stomach," or that rotten potatoes make me "turn up my nose," it is the emotion of disgust motivating our body to turn away from what might harm us. It is horrific and damaging when individuals feel disgust during contact with things or people who are causing them harm, yet still have to depend on that environment for their survival or well-being. If you are in a situation like this, seek help from a safe and trusted individual. Too often people with eating disorders feel disgust with themselves or their bodies. If such disgust drives you to turn away from yourself, mentally beat yourself up, harm yourself, or want to destroy or kill yourself, your disgust is leading you into, instead of away from, danger. Please get help.

Pride serves us well when it energizes and motivates us to build on our accomplishments. Eating disorders abuse pride, as they create a sense of identity and uniqueness in "being the best" at using eating disorder behaviors. Pride destroys people when they strive to do something better or be admired for things that cause harm to themselves or others. It is particularly harmful when emotions like love or happiness careen into emotions like shame, guilt, and anger. It is common for people with eating disorders to feel, for example, a spark of happiness, then immediately have the thought that they don't deserve or are not worthy to feel happy. This leads to feeling ashamed for feeling happy. This happens and you need to be on the lookout for it, catch it, and treat it because it will get in the way of recovery.

Your belief about hard emotions might be that they will drown and destroy you unless you find a way to stop them, speed them along, or push them down. Many of my clients speak of the benefits of eating, bingeing, purging, or restricting nutrition to control emotions. However, those benefits are short-lived, so the behaviors must be used often and used over and over again.

Thinking about an emotion doesn't mean that you try to stop it, understand what's wrong with you for having the emotion, or decry how weak you are or how you "should" feel instead. This makes them bigger. Since emotions are biological, being aware of our physical sensations is often our first clue that an emotion has shown up. We can also notice our thoughts, urges, statements, body language, and behaviors to understand what is happening emotionally. Once you notice the signals that an emotion is present, use the STOP tool. Emotions neither go away nor remain at the most extreme intensity forever, so the goal is to watch for changes in their intensity and to let your emotions, thoughts, and body settle down until you can get your logical, thinking brain back.

Know What's Running the Show
Eating Disorder Thought: "One thing you can trust is that people lie to you. Not many people are honest enough to tell you that you are disgusting to them."
Truth: Most of us have times when we think we know what someone is thinking about us. Most of us have times when we think others are judging our appearance. It is possible to know for sure what you think, believe, or intend; but, despite convincing thoughts to the contrary, it is impossible to know for certain what others think, believe, or intend.

Most people who struggle with eating disorders can become consumed with stories in their head, certain they know what others are thinking about them, and it is mostly negative. My clients regularly tell me about negative thoughts I have about them when I don't even know I'm having those thoughts. Can you see the error? Mind reading and personalizing can play a part in causing an eating disorder; the eating disorder then gives them a turbo boost that causes more stories about what others think about us, and the cycle takes on a life of its own.

To put this information about emotions into a coherent package, consider this example: An emotion typically starts when something happens. The event can be internal, like a thought about the future or a memory of the past. Or an emotion can be prompted by an external event, like getting passed over for a job. For example, my clients rattle off such automatic thoughts as, "I'm fat. Fat people don't get good jobs." "I don't deserve it anyway." "I'm a failure." "I'm stupid, fat, worthless, and ugly." "There's nothing about me that stands out." The list goes on and on. Do you recognize any of these thoughts as your own? If so, does it surprise you that these thoughts are more related to eating disorder thinking than unique to you? Interpretations about being defective both come from shame and create more shame. Shame pushes us to hide (avoid future auditions) or conform to be more desirable (get "skinny enough" in order to succeed). The eating disorder is firmly in control as dieting or compensating for calories becomes the path to accomplishing the goal, or binging or restricting is used to temporarily soothe the pain. This is how thoughts, urges, and behaviors can be dictated by ignored or overwhelming emotions.

Therefore, it is important for us to know when our emotions are running the show. It makes sense to have particular emotions in certain circumstances.

However, just because you have an emotion doesn't mean that it is motivating your thoughts or behaviors to do what is helpful to you in the situation. Step back, look at the facts, and challenge the eating disorder thoughts for yourself.

A thought is a thought. A flower is a flower. A feeling is a feeling. What you see with your eyes is what you see. An opinion or story about any of those things is merely an opinion about that thing. Just because you happen to have a thought, a feeling, an opinion, or a belief about something does not mean it is necessarily accurate. If you can see it, hear it, taste it, touch it, or smell it, you can be sure it's accurate because information from the world around you confirms it. For example, there is a difference between someone's eyebrows wrinkling together (which you can see) and that person being mad at you (a story your mind might create about the wrinkled brow). Some people wrinkle their brow when they have a headache or are concentrating. Like Robyn, your recovery depends on breaking free from the stories in your head. Your recovery journey depends, in part, on gradually exposing yourself to feelings in these ways in order to eventually trust that you can experience them without drowning in them.

Robyn always felt larger than she wanted to be, "fat," even at her thinnest. Therapists who specialize in working with eating disorder recovery have interventions that can help you check the accuracy of your own thoughts, beliefs, or perceptions about your body. Until then, the eating disorder can tell you whatever it decides, and you are at risk of thinking, "Oh, yes, you're right," when it is actually selling you poison and you are drinking it, no questions asked.

 As you are going about your life, pay attention for just one hour. Notice the stories in your head. Anytime you have a thought that goes beyond what you can directly see, hear, taste, touch, or smell, it is probably a story about the information coming into your brain. Use the STOP tool. Get curious about and count how many stories your mind creates during the course of that hour. Try not to beat yourself up about the stories you are having because our brains are made to have stories so they can efficiently draw conclusions.

The problem is that the conclusions aren't necessarily accurate. Use this tool to help you learn to see the difference between the facts you actually observe and the stories your brain adds.

Example: If you are in the mall and thinking that others are disgusted and think you are fat when they look at you, STOP. Get curious and carefully observe how many people you actually see looking at you and how many people's eyes move up and down or become fixed on your body. Some do. Yet many of my clients begin to learn that very few people even look at others, much less stare beyond a quick glance. Despite being convinced that you know the thoughts of other people, you cannot. You might need to keep track of how many people look at you versus how many don't. You need to have a count in order to factually determine whether it is ten, fifty, eighty, or one hundred percent of others. Otherwise, you are making up things in your mind about what is going on, and eating disorders thrive on the stories.

Even if you choose to listen to eating disorder thoughts and believe it about certain things, please don't let it insult your intelligence by falling for those things that could be proven false if you just took some time to carefully observe the incoming information and the stories in your head about it. Once you practice and get the hang of this skill, you, like Robyn, will feel that your thoughts and emotions are better managed, because your stories are better managed. Lilly is fortunate. Imagine what true power could manifest if mothers, fathers, families, friends, loved ones, and society could learn and pass on the skill of taking in the signals, then deliberately observing and naming them as a way to help themselves and others decrease and cope with painful emotions. Even if, just once, a painful emotion could be changed by exposing its misfiring, it is worth the time and effort.

Get into Your Right Mind
Eating Disorder Thought: "They are saying you need to do a better job at controlling your feelings and to stop the "stories" in your head. That's why I'm here for you. I tell you the truth about what people think about you when no one else will. I protect you."

Truth: Eating disorders are often about pushing feelings away, pushing them down, or giving them an outlet. We are not encouraging you to manage your feelings in any of these ways. And it is always a crapshoot when we think we know what others are thinking without them telling us.

Historically, people were often encouraged in therapy to change their thoughts in order to change their emotions. This approach can be helpful, yet many of my clients with a predisposition for emotional sensitivity, perfectionistic thinking, and putting themselves down (characteristics of people with eating disorders) wonder what's wrong with them when they can't just change their thoughts to get rid of an emotion. This is a large part of the reason DBT was developed and brain science continues to inform us of the many ways to shift emotions by changing our physical reactions through both body and thought-based practices. Trying to think differently in order to change painful emotions can be like trying not to think about the painful burning sensation in your hand after it gets burned. Acting differently is like putting ice on your hand to ease the pain, which helps you think about it less. *Actions* tend to change emotions more quickly than trying to change our *thoughts*. AFTER our actions begin to shift our emotions, it is less difficult to change our thoughts.

> **The benefits of working *with* instead of against our emotions are life-changing.**

When Robyn had the urge to avoid auditions because she felt too fat, she knew the emotion of shame was working against her. Her shame, gone unchecked, might have pushed her to restrict, purge, or avoid auditions until she was "skinny enough"—or all three. Robyn was mindful and saw the signals, and then observed her body, thoughts, and emotions and what they were urging her to do. She named what she was observing. Then she allowed all of the information to flow through her as she sorted the actual facts from the stories in her head. If an emotion is consuming you and getting you to think and do things that are not helpful in the situation, you might need to do something different. After observing and naming what she saw and heard as well as her resulting thoughts, Robyn could evaluate whether or not it was 100 percent guaranteed that her body was getting in the way of her getting every part. She realized that, instead, it was 100 percent guaranteed that her embarrassment and disgust for her body were the factors that stood between her and getting a part, as long as they kept her from even going to auditions. She knew that the only way to get a part, which was her goal, was to go to auditions anyway. Robyn began to suspect that waiting until she was "skinny enough" (based on the eating disorder's standards) to land a part would leave her hiding and avoiding auditions forever. What disastrous outcomes this would have caused for an actor! Leaving her eating disorder behavior at the door, Robyn took her determined, shame-filled body to the audition and immersed herself in her audition as if her life depended on it. The life Robyn dreamed of *did* depend on it.

Using her deliberately chosen response instead of her automatic reaction worked at a time when letting shame dictate her actions would only have gotten in the way. Robyn got the part. It confirmed that the emotion and the stories in her head weren't helpful (or accurate) after all. This is how Robyn's *action* of going to auditions even when she felt ashamed of her body helped lay the foundation for her recovery.

For fear that I am making this sound too easy, let me assure you that it is anything but easy, and it takes a lifetime of practice for all of us. It is worth the effort, as the benefits of working *with* instead of against our emotions are life-changing.

When you observe the signals, name them. It may or may not be best to harness and use their energy and influence to your advantage but you cannot know that without sorting facts from stories. Robyn knew that her anger at her eating disorder (for continuing its efforts to convince her that her value and worth were based on the size and shape of her body) was helpful. She used her anger for energy to develop and act on a plan for what she would do differently when her eating disorder went after her with its emotional club.

A plan of action can be developed for any pattern or reaction that is predictable. This can help you override your initial urge in favor of a more useful response when one is needed. Because Robyn's pattern was so predictable, it was preventable. As Robyn put her plan into action, it focused her anger toward uncovering her worth in ways more in line with her actual goals and values. That's when she began to see her anger overpowering the last of the emotional hold that the eating disorder had on her. It was Robyn's willingness to work *with* her anger that pried the last remaining tentacles of her eating disorder from around her heart and finally freed her from its grasp. With practice and mindfulness, loosening the eating disorder's grasp on you is possible for you also.

What *Really* Protects You?

Eating Disorder Thought: "No brainer. Me, of course! I'm the only one who really has your back. I protect you. Stick with me because you can't trust anyone else to protect you."

Truth: There are ways to protect yourself, to keep situations from hitting you as hard emotionally *and* to cope with difficult emotions once they hit. Those ways have nothing to do with the illusions and quick fixes your eating disorder uses to "protect" you from emotions.

Hopefully you are beginning to see that emotions often happen before we have the chance to influence them. However, there are things you can do to ward off or decrease the impact that difficult emotions have on you. Stabilize your nutrition using your registered dietitian and structured eating plan as resources, rather than the eating disorder, making sure you take in nutritional fuel every four hours. Work to treat or manage physical pain, illness, and health issues, including vision and dental problems, as well as getting routine preventive care. Prescription or over-the-counter medications, herbs, or supplements can affect emotions so pay attention to how they affect you. Use these only as prescribed or as directed on the label.

One alcoholic beverage makes it harder to see the signals, accurately assess information, and respond deliberately. I am not preaching against drinking alcohol; I am encouraging you to avoid it when you need to figure out how to respond deliberately to emotional situations. Get as much sleep as you need and no more than necessary. Sleep medications, though sometimes necessary, create low-quality sleep. If you are willing to work at it, there are many ways to promote the kind of sleep that is most beneficial. Look into those, with professional help if needed, and experiment to see if they are helpful to you. Physical activity within the guidelines set by your physician and nutritionist can improve mood. Too much or a lack of physical activity is also hard on your emotions. It is all about balance. Don't let painful emotions build up, and maintain regular interaction with other people. If you are out of balance (deprived or in excess) in any of these areas, it could explain why you are having more difficulty with emotions at a particular time, and balancing where you can is helpful.

Challenge yourself but make sure you see and take in your accomplishments. (Dieting, weight loss, and the like don't count!) Doing big and small things you enjoy while paying attention to what you're doing—and your mood while you are doing it—is important. Remember or consider your goals, values, and priorities, aside from anything related to food or your body, and let those guide your actions. Create a daily gratitude practice. These are the things that also help you build a foundation and understanding of how to find and strengthen your sense of self.

Remember, too, that we are talking about freedom of emotion, not freedom *from* emotion. It will take time for your brain to learn that emotions are not your enemy. So take a deep breath, slow down, open your eyes, involve yourself in your life, balance your life, and learn how to get from the life raft to the shore.

Can you hear the calling?
It is the calling of purpose.
We all have it. We all can live it.
Shhh . . . listen.
Make a change.

Today, I will take time to remind myself of the gifts
I was brought into the world with. If I don't know,
I will allow myself to think of something positive
about myself, pushing through the noise of the eating
disorder until I find it. I will then put those gifts out
into the universe where they belong and be willing
to utilize them when the invitation arises. If the
eating disorder says no, I will ask, "Why not?"—
reminding myself that it is I who has the choice.
—Robyn

7.

Gather Your Support Team

Spanish Pay Phones and Glaswegian Nightclubs

By Robyn

I loved to act. Ever since I can remember, acting was what it was all about for me. I still feel that way, even though I am not doing it any longer. At age two, I often took my mum and neighbor hostage and made them sit through my incoherent improvisations, full of mumbling but also undeniable commitment. When I was a teenager, I would often spend my lunchtime writing my own scripts and then perform them later that day in my acting class. It was my passion, and it sprang from a deep, tangible desire to move people.

When I was nineteen, a Tony Award-winning British director came to Sydney, Australia to watch a small co-op play that his friend had directed. I happened to be in it. I was raw, but ready. The director asked me to audition for his film. It was an adaptation of Anthony Chekhov's play, *Uncle Vanya*. And just like that, I found myself cast as Violet the housemaid. It was the start to that dream I had fervently believed in from the age of all of two. At twenty-four, I had a series on TV. It was my first ongoing job, playing Shay McWilliams for 56 episodes. By twenty-six, after much persuasion from friends who had already gone before me, I headed to where I believed big dreams could come true: Hollywood. But by then, the disorder had taken over (meaning there was little room in my life for anything else,) and no matter what extraordinary opportunities came to me—and I was blessed with many dream-making opportunities—they never were more important than the eating disorder. *When I get thin enough, I will concentrate on my career. When I get thin enough, I'll show the world who I really am.* The dreams my two-year-old self had continued to manifest were eaten up by the disorder that was ever so hungry for *more—always more.*

Although I was never able to see the gifts in my life, partly due to the negative thoughts of the disorder and partly due to my temperament, I always had people who believed in me and wanted to love me, if I would have let them.

I believed that if I opened up, people would see my insides—the confusion, the fear, and a story that would have them judging me and running for the hills. I worked my whole life to create a persona that disguised my truth. It was the acting gig of my life!

I made decisions based on how I felt. Unfortunately, most of the time I felt unworthy and "less than." I told my new manager (who had been sending casting agents chocolates and flowers just to goad them into seeing this new Aussie actor) that I would return in six months to pick up on the opportunities he had worked so hard to create for me. I didn't return for five years. Needless to say, the opportunities were gone.

Within those five years, still running from my truth, I traveled back to Australia, then London and Spain, and landed in Scotland. Seeking perfection in whatever I did, I'd made a decision to study at a highly regarded Scottish music and drama academy to perfect my acting technique. I went to school with a group of people who were doing the Master's degree so that they could do the kind of work I'd already done. I did it because I never felt good enough. I ran to seven countries in five years, and the eating disorder followed me.

In the middle of the night on the hauntingly dark streets of Valencia, Spain, where I had taken a position in children's theatre as a way to run away from myself again, I sobbed into a pay phone to my mother, whom I had woken from her sleep. "I can't do this anymore. I can't live like this." She knew I was desperate and trapped in the disorder. It wasn't her first rodeo with the disorder either. She had been by my side since the age of sixteen when she first found out about it. She too felt powerless. This disorder is a heartbreaking experience for parents and loved ones too. I had been bingeing and purging my way through Spain, spending up to six hours a day in the bathroom. I was unable to stop, unable to embrace anything outside of my disorder. I think my mum was okay with getting the middle-of-the-night calls because she believed that the alternative (not getting them) would mean the death of her child.

In Spain, it was not uncommon to perform two to three shows a day, eating out for all meals. One day our driver was running late and our lunch break was cut short as we piggybacked shows. I had consumed the menu of the day and a carafe of cheap red wine, which I planned to purge. But to my dismay, the driver rushed us from the restaurant before I had time to rid myself of the meal I would have never eaten if I couldn't purge. All the way back to the theatre, I was fretting about what I would do. I felt panicked and obsessed. Upon returning to the theatre, I found a bucket in the bathrooms and placed it behind the stage, so that when I returned after each scene, I could purge. I would run on stage as Blue-Hat Betty, with my bulging waist and bloated face, then run backstage and purge as Robbed-of-All-Dignity Robyn. Yet to many, it appeared I was living the dream.

I had learned how to cope by trying to get whatever I could to ease my discomfort at the very moment that emotional smarting began. Looking back, I did a great many things in my disorder that caused me shame and annihilated all things good in my life. Most of all, though, when I think back to what caused me the most shame when I was in my disorder, it was the way I treated my "person," my beloved Mum. She would have sacrificed anything for me— including her own recovery. Yes, families need their own recovery too.

One of the things that caused me great shame was the fact that I got my mum to pay an international fee of $30,000 from her home savings so that I could be encouraged to go on living.

I told Mum that attending the Music and Drama Academy would provide something worth living for. I *believed* this. I felt like an imposter, a fraud. I thought, and insisted to my mum, that getting the proper education instead of passing over it due to my qualifying experience would make me feel legitimate. News flash, nothing would have made me feel legitimate or worthy while in the clutches of an eating disorder. I would never be enough. Nonetheless, back then I was convinced this move would bring me some relief from the eating disorder's accusations that I was merely a fraud who deserved nothing. I insisted this would lessen my misery at the hands of the eating disorder. She prayed it would free me from the depths of my agony, and in turn bring her some freedom from her darkest fears of completely losing her daughter. I could have waited a year and paid a sixth of this fee, as I would then have been classified as a resident of the United Kingdom. But I couldn't wait; I wouldn't wait, nor would the eating disorder. I needed something to focus on and to bring me hope, something to project my fantasies upon.

My mum never gave up hope on me, even when she'd grown weary of seeing a stranger who had the facial features (despite the swollen, ripped blood vessels in my eyes) of her child that she loved so dearly and profoundly. She had long ago lost the daughter that she raised, but she so desperately wanted her back. And like most parents, she was willing to go to any lengths—and any cost—to make that happen. If I could take back the pain I caused my mum, dear God, I would. It has taken a great deal of work to understand and forgive myself for the hurt I have caused others and not had a chance to make amends for fully. Having had my own daughters in recovery, I see even more clearly my mum's love for me, and the way she was willing to fight like Muhammad Ali alongside me. In the name of unbridled, fierce momma love, I'd do the same thing for my daughters. I think my mum would be proud. She wouldn't want me wasting my time in shame. I can imagine her saying, "You've done it long enough. It's time now, Robbie. It's time."

◆ ◆ ◆

The more I isolated myself in my disorder, the more it tightened its grip upon me. I would never be perfect, and nor would the life I lived. It didn't matter what acting gig I got, what education level I achieved, or what size my thighs were—it would never ever be good enough. After all, perfection is not something that you can ever achieve within an eating disorder. Perfection for the eating disorder is being dead. To expose the lie of perfection, I needed to expose the disorder that was pushing the lies like painkillers on the black market. To expose the disorder, I had to expose my part.

The powerful stigma of an eating disorder (a mental illness) was always just under the surface. I had an ugly secret that, if uncovered, would reveal my vulnerability for the entire world to see. But this very thing, if I allowed it to be exposed, would open me to the life I had been seeking through my running. That vulnerability is now my strength. That, coupled with acceptance in knowing that I could no longer do it alone, was the key that unshackled me from the burden of my ugly secret. It was true that I could never do it alone, and nothing I did could change that. It came down to sharing my story and asking for help . . . or dying.

After midnight, as I lay defeated in my bed in the heart of Glasgow, I listened to the raucous sound of two drunken Glaswegian men declaring their strength as they threw punches at each other just outside my window. It wasn't unusual for this type of scene to be the soundtrack to my weekend. I lived across from a popular nightclub that would start gathering steam in the wee hours of the morning. I would usually drown out the racket with earplugs, which were scattered around the narrow room covered in rich, purple wallpaper that hid me from the eyes of others and aided my ability to binge in secret. But on this winter-chilled night, I decided to forgo the earplugs so the sound of the nightclub would shield me from the noise inside my head. Somehow, the pounding of fists and the men's loyal friends egging them on seemed more pleasant to me than my own thoughts. I'd been drinking, and only moments before I'd been weeping on the yellow pages of the phonebook, which was open to reveal the number of the suicide hotline.

I lay on the floor, unable to balance myself when standing, and slid my hand to the phone that sat on the black, crumb-sprinkled carpet, as if it were waiting for me. But instead of calling the hotline, I called a friend from the support group I had attended a week before out of a desperate need to find a solution to this horrid disorder. The support group had provided me with a phone list that I would normally have thrown out after it had remained wrinkled in my handbag for weeks, collecting the crumbs from each of my binges. But this night in Glasgow, I chose to share my story with a person with whom I identified. I felt safe with her because I had witnessed her openly sharing her own story with a group that supported recovery and honored truth, and it gave me the courage to do the same.

I chose to start telling my truth to those who identified with me and wanted to help me, and in whom I trusted. This act changed my life forever.

Calling for Backup

By Espra

Eating Disorder Thought: "You don't need anyone. You don't need to tell anyone. If you tell people about this, they will think you are crazy and look at you differently. They may even try to control you."
Truth: You cannot do this alone.

The eating disorder takes a toll on relationships. Still, gathering some help to help you fight the eating disorder is critical. Here we've outlined the things that are important to consider and to ask of others when you are working to create a necessary safety net for your survival and for your recovery.

Medical Care

While the eating disorder will tell you that it is unnecessary and that it is not that bad, and that others will laugh because you are not sick at all, tell your medical provider the truth about your eating disorder and symptoms anyway. Your urge will be to downplay the severity and frequency of your behaviors and symptoms. Don't. It will keep you from recovery. Find a physician who can assess your physical health status using the correct labs, cardiac, and other tests, then help you monitor and manage your physical health and medical needs. Start by having a thorough medical assessment by a provider who is familiar with the many medical risks associated with eating disorders as soon as possible. If your physician is willing but needs additional information about medical evaluation and management of eating disorders, take them a copy of the Academy for Eating Disorders (AED) websites' educational report on recognizing and managing the medical risks for individuals with eating disorders, which is available for reading or to download. Let them know the American Medical Association (AMA) website also has an educational video on screening and managing eating disorders that was developed in conjunction with the National Eating Disorder Association (NEDA) and AED.

Make sure your physician does not focus exclusively on body mass index or weight to diagnose the severity of your eating disorder and to determine appropriate medical interventions. **Eating disorders cannot be diagnosed based on weight or body size.** Make sure the focus of stabilizing the eating disorder does not include a weight-loss plan. While eating disorders love this, it does not lead to recovery. Ask your physician if he or she is willing to coordinate your care with your other providers. Make a plan for the frequency and types of measures that will be needed in order to monitor your medical status. If you can find a physician who is willing and able to take this approach to assessing and helping you manage your eating disorder, you are well on your way.

 Write down all your symptoms and eating disorder behaviors. Then look over your list and honestly evaluate it for accuracy. Identify what you have left out or minimized and correct it now. Take a deep breath and take this list with you to your physician's visit. Be sure to give the list to your physician.

Faith and Finding a Power Greater Than Ourselves

Living in the throes of an eating disorder creates a spiritual crisis. It can rob your spirit, your essence, and it can compromise your long-term values. Any self-respect or self-esteem you had plummets and shame takes over. A twelve-step group like Eating Disorders Anonymous can help you heal a life of obsession by, in part, aligning with a "higher power." While some people use the phrase "a power greater than ourselves," "higher power" can be wherever you find strength such as the group itself, nature, consciousness, existential freedom, God, the universe, Mother Earth, science, Buddha, or anything that is greater than you alone and is also loving and caring. Seek your own source of strength, even if it is unclear right now, and use it, while you accept others as they do the same. Take what works for you and leave the rest. If a local Eating Disorders Anonymous Group does not exist in your area, you can start one by first going to their website.

Other Support Groups

A local eating disorder facility or one of your healthcare providers may be able to give you referrals for support groups in your area. Weight-loss groups are *not* what you need. Therapy groups that target identity development, assertiveness training, and general quality of life skills can be helpful. Make sure that their focus is sensitive to the needs of those with eating disorders. Look for groups that are led by a registered dietitian or therapist who specializes in working with eating disorders.

Check out a group by attending two or three meetings before you commit, and be wary of discussions, advice, people, and anything else that can trigger your eating disorder thoughts and behaviors. Attend groups that seem helpful to your recovery, and stay away from those that don't.

Find groups that teach and support one another in practicing mindfulness, meditation, and yoga. Hot yoga does not count. It will be more harmful than helpful to your body and recovery.

Mental Health Therapy

Both the National Eating Disorder Association (NEDA) and International Association of Eating Disorder Professionals foundation (IAEDP) websites have directories to help you find a therapist in your area with specialized training in eating disorder treatment. If a provider is not available, contact the nearest eating disorder treatment program that might be able to give you referral information. If the above options leave you empty-handed, ask your regular medical provider or other professionals for referrals. In beginning therapy, it is important to have some level of comfort with a therapist's knowledge of eating disorder treatment and a sense of rapport or connection with them. Ask about the therapist's eating disorder education and training, the frequency and amount of continuing education they do on the subject of eating disorders, and how many other clients they see or have seen with eating disorder issues. Don't presume they are a specialist because their advertisement says they treat eating disorders. Ideally, a therapist will work as a team with your medical provider and nutritionist, so that each professional can focus on their role in helping you recover. You can also get the most out of your therapy sessions if you and your therapist focus on the mental health aspects of your recovery and leave the food part primarily to your registered dietitian.

Therapists who discuss dieting or "good/bad" foods will not be your best allies for your recovery journey.

Nutritional Therapy

You need nutritional therapy with a registered dietitian (RD) who is skilled in treating eating disorders. Ask at your local hospital or eating disorder program or look in your local phonebook for referrals. Be aware. Weight-loss counseling or focusing on "good and bad foods," no matter how badly you might want it, will not lead to eating disorder recovery.

Ask dietitians how much training and education they have in eating disorder treatment, how many eating disorder clients they have, and what approach they use. Look for a dietitian who works with intuitive or mindful eating. Though face-to-face sessions are ideal, it is more important that you find a dietitian skilled in treating eating disorders, and one that you are convinced has a philosophical approach that is in the best interest of your recovery. If there are none in your area, you can find dietitians who do nutritional counseling via computer or phone.

Informal Support

Eating disorders are mind-boggling to most people. Look around at the people in your life. You can probably identify those who are able to support and help you in the ways that you need support and help. These individuals might be among your immediate family, extended family, and friends. They may be people you know from school, a place of faith, or many other places. Do not let your eating disorder make this decision by choosing people to help you who will glamorize or fuel the eating disorder.

Look for those who, rather than rushing to give advice or problem solve, can listen, encourage, talk about emotions more than food, and are not critical about their bodies or yours. It is best if they seem to eat from a mindset that does not include rules about types or amounts of foods that are okay to eat. Anyone who focuses on body size, shape and weight, dieting, and critiquing food choices will not help your recovery efforts. Empathy and compassion are key. Talk to them about how they can support you, and decide with them how that support can be put into action. Most of all, be honest with them and teach them what you need and how to give it to you.

People also find sources of strength in members of the clergy, prayer, meditation, knowledgeable lay people, and reading. Make sure that the focus is on healing and forgiveness and not condemnation.

Eating Disorders Anonymous (EDA) can be an amazingly helpful path. It is a twelve-step program that is not based on what you do or do not eat, but focuses on where you find your strength and how to access it and heal yourself as well as the toxic emotions, like the shame, guilt, and self-disgust, that only hold you back.

Family Portrait

Among the predisposing genetic factors that make a person vulnerable to developing an eating disorder are a highly sensitive emotional nature, a perfectionistic nature, and a people-pleasing nature. Recognize these as valuable, but as vulnerabilities when seeking support relationships.

You are seeking environmental and family support that can be helpful parts of your recovery. There may be family relationship factors that play a part in your difficulties. If so, in a structured therapy setting, discuss with family members things that they have done, not done, said, or not said that have been hurtful to you and how they can help now. Also, if you have relationships with particular family members where you feel a level of safety that will allow you to hear the same from them, using therapy to address these issues can be valuable as well. The "gold" in this work is in creating an environment where both of you can seek and make amends, invite and express forgiveness, repair relationships, and make changes where it is possible to do so.

Make decisions about when and how to do these things with care, thought, and the assistance of your therapist, as interactions like this do not always go as we wish, and you must be prepared to handle that. You and your therapist can identify those family members who can play an active role in your healing and recovery and figure out how to teach them how they can help you. Ask them for exactly what you need.

Some family members may not be the best members for your recovery support team. For example, individuals who struggle themselves, trigger your eating disorder thoughts and behaviors, or who have difficulty making sense of your eating disorder are not your best recovery allies. In these cases, you may need to work with your therapist to figure out how to navigate these relationships in ways that protect your recovery efforts as much as possible.

Notice if there is someone in your family who expresses consistent guilt that they may have caused the eating disorder. You are at risk of hiding your feelings in an attempt to protect this person's emotions. The best thing to do here is to help that family member find a therapist who works with eating disorders and/or a support group for themselves. Once you trust that your family member is working to understand and heal their pain, you can focus on your own recovery instead of trying to take care of their pain and guilt.

 Find someone in your environment with whom you can be honest about your eating disorder behaviors. Decide how often you will check in with this person, what you will discuss, and how you need them to respond. Example: Most of my clients plan a ten-minute check-in with their support person every one to two days. Write down three to five questions that you will address each time you meet. Examples: Did you binge today? What emotions have you experienced today? What three things did you try to use before you binged? What non-eating disordered behaviors did you use today that were helpful? Did you eat three meals today? Did you do anything to spend calories since we last spoke?

Move forward where you can, as no benefit comes from blaming or guilt. Heal what is realistic and appropriate to heal, with individuals who can help you. You might increase interaction with some family members and decrease interaction with others, based on what is in the best interest of your recovery right now. Make these decisions deliberately, with your therapist, as no benefit comes from rehashing the past or continuously asking, "Why?"

As you gather your troops and train them to help you fight the eating disorder and defend your progress, remember this: You need to find as many supporters as possible. You, like anyone else, cannot be perfect. It is impossible to move towards recovery without mistakes and slips. You must find those with whom you can be honest about what is going on with your eating disorder and your recovery. The eating disorder will discourage you from being honest when you make mistakes. It is yet another lie that mistakes are something to be ashamed of and hidden. Mistakes are part of recovery, as well as part of being human. Recovery is made up of admitting our mistakes to those who can help us, exploring where we could have done things differently, and making a plan to address it. Recovery is not about perfection, but realizing that you are off track and turning back toward your recovery path as quickly as possible, using your growing arsenal of skills. In fact, that's the best any of us humans can do when we make mistakes. So gather your troops, train them, have plans to correct tactical errors, and head into battle with your troops around you.

Some days our pain and fear can feel unbearable, and although the eating disorder behavior is also intolerable, it is oh-so-familiar. But there is another way. We can turn to trusting friends, a higher power, or a support network in order to move forward within our recovery.

Today, what we can't do alone we can do together.
—*Robyn*

8.

Let's Build a New Plan

Cold Steel Chairs and the Powerful Truth

By Robyn

Fear is palpable and expresses itself in many forms. There was the raw fear that would shoot through my body with electrical force and break through every cell of my being until it reached my mind. Then there was the manipulative kind of fear, which had me disguising my truth to get whatever I needed from others or myself so I could be okay in my own skin. And then there was the fear I despised the most and hid from at any cost—the vulnerable kind of fear. Even the thought of having to live through the process of being vulnerable petrified me. It was like sitting on a cold steel chair stark naked on an illuminated stage in front of the whole world, where the lights revealed the very essence of me. Vulnerability was unacceptable to me, so I hid.

I hid within the familiarity of the eating disorder. I was not weak or stupid, nor "bad"; in fact, when I first found the behavior of the eating disorder, I was a clever little person to have discovered it. As an anxious, sad, and confused eleven-year old, I put on my superhero cape and panties and rescued myself from emotions that my young mind could not fathom. The eating disorder behavior was my salvation, my solution, and medication that numbed me enough to survive in a world where I thought my mum was dying. It provided me shelter from the growing pains of life, and sometimes it even brought me joy, hope, and a sense of identity—even accomplishment.

I am grateful to that little girl for doing all that she could to get me through life. I survived. I thank her. If I were to revisit her, I'd see her in her bedroom bingeing, an act of relief, much like I imagine a hardworking mother might relax with a glass of wine or a magazine after putting her children to bed. She would take a breath. This is her time; she has made it through another day of caring for others. Just as I, the little girl, felt as I stuffed myself with anything I could.

◆ ◆ ◆

My mother's eyes were black, sunken circles, as if she had been beaten with a perfectly circular object. Her body was wilting; we could see her color and vivaciousness drying up before us. There at the dining table at 7 Sadie Avenue, just after I closed my eyes to pretend that my Brussels sprouts were ice cream in order to eat them, my mother told us what the doctor had strongly suggested: "I have lupus." By the end of the night, we heard, "I may be dying." In her own state of vulnerability, and fighting for her life as her kidneys threatened to fail, she had spoken the words that changed my life and had me dreading her death for nineteen years. These were words she regretted saying to us for the rest of her life.

The debilitating fear of losing my mum played out in my mind like a Brothers Grimm fairytale. I would find myself envisioning her death over and over. In my child's mind, I believed unequivocally that when my mum died, I would die also. I would picture myself—face up, arms spread out across her glossy, black coffin—asking the priest to bury me along with her. I imagined rock particles piercing my flesh as the sun shone through the old gum trees like the hands of God calling out for us both. I had a great need to externalize my emotional pain, and this image, along with my dramatic flair, satisfied that. Soon after, my bingeing replaced that horrid vision's place.

Fear is such a primal thing, a human trait that no one is excluded from. It serves us, as it prepares our bodies to run from danger. But when there is no actual danger and fear begins to dictate our actions and thrust us into greater danger—danger we embrace—there is something that requires our attention. My mum often asked me to do what I knew I needed to do to recover from the eating disorder, just as she did what she needed to do by taking her medicine, changing her diet, and meditating to stop the progression of her lupus. With a profound commitment to live, Mum tried everything and anything to stay alive. She not only lived for another nineteen years, she showed me how to live fully and deliberately. I wanted to do that too.

When recovery commences, the fear and other negative emotions that come with being human do not cease. We cannot simply put down the behavior and get on with life as if nothing ever happened. My mum had to deal with the fear of dying and the unacceptable possibility as a mother having to abandon her children. Then when her disease finally went into remission, she had to face her family's fear, as well as her own, that one day the disease could resurface.

Any recovery process encourages us to face emotions that were there already, and are then enhanced in recovery. There are many emotions to sweep out from under the rug, and life is going to get messier before it gets cleaned up. But rest assured, recovery will create a safe place to examine all of these emotions and put them in their rightful places so that we can live full and deliberate lives.

It is said that our truth will set us free. Acknowledging my story and honoring it has brought me much freedom. The little girl in me did what she did to keep me alive; but as an adult, I get to make better choices in how to live. It is no longer okay for me to simply survive and stuff down my fear.

The shelter of the eating disorder also sheltered me from the full life that I now explore. When I got into recovery, I had to put on the superhero cape and panties once again and bid farewell to the eating disorder. Bit by bit, the eating disorder's power began to fade with every truth I told myself. I learned how to redirect my fear to be heard instead of hidden within the eating disorder. Although sometimes, when I feel exposed or vulnerable, it has been difficult not to hide, I have continued to choose comfort in support, pausing, and saying no to the illusive quick fixes that our culture loves to force feed us.

Now, long into my recovery, in a place in which I do not give much thought to the eating disorder unless sharing my story, I can still see how my fear can get in the way of living fully if I allow it. I wish it wouldn't; it has a terrible tendency to make things so much harder and slow my process down. But when I question the facts, listen and speak from my truth, and am willing to let go of the ruminating fear, I can move toward a life of freedom that I know has my name all over it . . . and sometimes, that's the hardest thing I have to do.

How to Honor Your Fear and Seek Your Truth

By Espra

Being Brutally Honest with Yourself

Eating Disorder Thought: "Robyn had a reason to have an eating disorder. Her mother was very sick. You don't have problems like that. You're just weak." Or, if you have had some sort of specific trauma that you can put your finger on, "You are making things up, imagining them as worse than they actually were to justify having an eating disorder."

Truth: Regardless of why the eating disorder came into being, we know that when individuals lack the skills or opportunity within their environments to honor the fact that they have emotional pain, there is an increased risk of developing an eating disorder. Either way, with or without clear traumatic events, an individual needs access to validation by others of the impact of their experiences. In this way individuals learn to validate themselves, increasing their ability to heal from difficult emotional experiences.

Robyn hid. She hid from others and from herself. As with Robyn, it is likely that the vulnerability and honesty you need in order to question the role of your eating disorder and why you need it in your life have become the very enemies you'd do anything to hide from. Being brutally honest with yourself about what the eating disorder brings you (harmful and helpful) can be terrifying. An eating disorder would not have become your solution to coping if you had a less destructive, less complicated way that worked.

A common function of an eating disorder is to help cope with emotional fear and pain in some way. Its incessant chatter might distract you from more frightening thoughts and emotions. Eating disorder obsessions and behaviors often bring welcome relief, in a miserably comforting sort of way, as they leave little time or energy to think of other worries. They bring avoidance and distraction. Hope arises as the eating disorder promises lottery-sized returns of true happiness, self-worth, acceptance, or protection from judgment if you embrace it. It may communicate your inner pain outwardly or give you a sense of control in a terrifying world. Whatever the benefits seem to be, for many, the eating disorder seems to do a wonderful job, in an immediate sense, before it ultimately robs you of everything.

The eating disorder convincingly presents itself as the only voice of total honesty about your defectiveness and flaws, telling you how to compensate for, conceal, or divert attention from them. It will say that shoving your body into a particular weight, shape, or size is a brilliant, unique solution to avoid judgment, criticism, and risk of not fitting in.

Unique, my ass! It is a big, fat lie! How about saying, "Brilliant, eating disorder, a unique solution just for me and eleven million other people in America. You're making me feel pretty special now." To be alive is to feel vulnerable, and it is unavoidable.

Do you think you don't have a good enough reason to feel emotional pain and fear? You might be terrified to admit that you carry emotional burdens, judging yourself and fearing judgment from others that you are weak or wanting attention. Healing and recovery start with admitting that you carry emotional pain that scares the crap out of you. No matter how insignificant you think it is, whether you brought it on yourself or it was heaped upon you, whether you deserve it or not, you must take the terrifying step of getting honest about whatever your bottom-line fear might be.

Eating disorders are usually about coping with pain and fear in the best way you can find. It's safe to assume that if you had the skills to cope with pain and fear outright, you would have done it that way. Most people are not taught those skills, as families rarely know them to teach. You need to stop lying to yourself about why you use the eating disorder. Find your truth and target the bottom line of this disorder with a new plan.

What is it that you would like to feel more than anything in the world? Caution: "Skinny, size ___, small enough thighs, cheeks that aren't 'chubby,' not hungry, in control," are not the right answers. Skinny is not an emotion. Fat is not an emotion. As loud, strong, and miserable as they are, they are not emotions; they are thoughts.

Ask yourself, "What is it that I crave to feel more than anything in the world?" When an answer pops into your mind, follow up with the question, "And if I felt that, what would happen?" Keep asking that question until you get to the bottom of what you really, truly crave. When you believe that you have gotten down to your core emotional craving, write it down. Just by doing this you are practicing courage in being vulnerable and honest. You are fighting the eating disorder.

Example: "More than anything in the world I want to feel successful. And if I were successful, what would happen? I'd lose weight. And if I lost weight, what would happen? I'd be skinny. And if I were skinny? I could be outgoing. And if I were outgoing? I could meet people and feel like I belong . . . I would feel included . . . I wouldn't feel all alone." That's it. You wouldn't feel all alone. That's your truth.

You'll know when you get there. You may find yourself sighing, dropping your shoulders, relaxing, or getting teary, to name a few physical clues. The profound words and voice of wise eating disorder psychodrama expert and teacher, Mary Bellofatto, MA, LMHC, ring in my head as she once told me, "You know . . . that you know . . . that you know." (Think about that.) Then she said, "And you pretend that you don't know." I've learned through practicing this, both myself and with my clients, that Mary's right. We know when we've hit our core truth, and while trembling at the thought, we need to trust it.

The good news is that there are specific skills you can learn to cope with hard emotions without the negative consequences that an eating disorder brings. Please trust that there are more options to living your life than your eating disorder (one extreme) and not acting on your eating disorder in exchange for a life of misery (the other extreme). As you consider this, you, like Robyn, begin to take back your power and use it to build a life worth being a part of.

Question Your Control

Eating Disorder Thought: "With me, you have control over something. YOU control how much or how little you eat or how many calories you do or do not keep in your body. Or you control when you lose control, and that's the ultimate control."

As we described in Chapter Five, despite the illusion of control, you have little to no power in your daily life with an eating disorder. Start owning that truth. You can turn your mindset from control to authentic power by being honest about rituals, binges, purges, nutritional restriction, and other self-destructive activities. Who and what are really controlling your behavior? If the eating disorder is your answer to being in perfect control, why is the power so short-lived, and why are you feeling unhappy enough to search for answers in this book?

Eating disorder behaviors can keep you safe from fear for about as long as it takes to engage in them. Then fear returns. Find safety in learning how to navigate your emotions in ways that last beyond the moment by allowing a healthy and functional flow of emotions, versus battling to numb or fight them off. They need not become a wall of pressure (that you need more and more eating disorder behaviors to hold back) or a consuming flood (in which you need more and more eating disorder behaviors to keep from drowning). As you begin to navigate the river and flow with its current, neither fighting to go faster nor resisting in an attempt to stop, you begin to build skills and faith that you can cope with emotions and even value them and their intended function of helping you.

The truth is, the more you avoid emotions by using eating disorder behavior, the more you become convinced that you are incapable of coping in any other way. This is how an eating disorder that seemed to bring perfect control begins to take on a life of its own, making you more and more out of control.

Take a Step Back and Take Back the Power

Eating Disorder Thought: "You need me. I numb the pain. You can't cope with pain without me."

Truth: Yes, your eating disorder serves as a quick fix for hard emotions . . . before it takes everything from you. And it *will* take everything from you.

Take a long, hard look at what humans actually have control over: Yourself, your interests, your journey, your day-to-day behavior, your values, how you interact with and love those around you, and how you show up for life. You are not in control. Despite what the eating disorder says, you are powerless. The eating disorder is running your life. If you don't believe me, think about a time when you decided to stop your eating disorder behaviors. Think about the thoughts and emotions that slammed you as you tried to do it. How long did it last? How long were you able to use sheer willpower and white-knuckle your way through stopping eating disorder behaviors? If not for the eating disorder, would you choose to feel out of control when you eat, exercise so hard or long as to interfere with other areas of your life, spend so much money on food, or put your head into a toilet? When I put it like that, does it spark some doubt about who or what is really in control of your life?

The other side of this coin is related to the nature of addiction. People in the throes of addiction, eating disorders included, are convinced their behaviors are veiled in secrecy and affect no one else. This is another lie. Others in your life who are being affected by your mindset and actions are, more than likely, afraid to bring up their concerns about your struggles or the impact of your behaviors on them. Meanwhile, the shame of engaging in such behaviors makes it seem impossible to talk about with others. The veil of secrecy lives on. It is rare that family members, friends, or loved ones of someone with an eating disorder are not aware of some aspect of the disorder, are not affected by it, and/or are not concerned about its effects. Sadly, it is also rare that loved ones can break through their own fears to bring up their concerns about eating disorder behaviors for discussion. If they do muster the courage to do so, it is rare that eating disorder sufferers can admit to themselves or others that there is indeed a problem. We just don't know how to talk about the hard stuff. Others do not know how to tell you they are worried that you stay home every night instead of being social, only eat lettuce without dressing, excuse yourself immediately and disappear after eating, or deplete their money or snack food supplies.

Start by getting honest with yourself about the many ways the eating disorder dictates your life. This will help you get honest about how the eating disorder creates more of the very pain it promises to get rid of.

 Get paper with a lot of room for writing and make a list. List everything you can recall that you have lied about related to your size, shape, weight, what you have eaten, or what you have not eaten. Write down things you tell others to divert suspicion, plus any instances of betrayal or stealing or violating your own values. Be sure to write down anything that comes to mind that the eating disorder says is not a big deal, for it most likely is.

Examples: "I told my husband that I had to go visit a sick friend so I could binge." "I told my friends that I had a huge exam the next day to avoid eating out." "I told my date that I had already eaten in order to eat as little as possible without it being suspicious." "I stole food." "I stole money to buy food." "I ate food from a dumpster."

Robyn found freedom in being truthful with herself, then with others. As you begin to be honest with yourself about what is happening, and then with carefully selected others, you begin to heal. The lies and feelings of needing the eating disorder to cope start to fade. As you build a pattern of truthfulness with yourself and then with others, even about your fears, a light will appear in the darkness of the recesses of your heart. Like Robyn, you

> **The grand illusion of the eating disorder is that it protects you from pain.**

will feel exposed and want to run to your eating disorder to protect you with its lies. As you redirect your fear and let yourself be heard in safe places, the fear gradually lessens, and you can find comfort in authentic support, learning to see quick fixes and old solutions as short-lived. The grand illusion of the eating disorder is that it protects you from pain. The reality is that nothing erases pain for good. Recovery alone does not stop the river of scary emotions any more than changing old, ineffective patterns stops them. Your goal must be to protect yourself by learning to navigate hard emotions, a process that actually decreases the pain in and of itself.

Let Robyn's story inspire you to see that allowing yourself to experience the hard emotions that are part of all of our journeys on this earth is what builds the safe container in which to sort, make sense of, and learn to work with them.

Just so you know, fear gets in the way of all of us, me included. I feel validated by Robyn's understanding of what pain does to her, as well as to the rest of us. I feel inspired by Robyn's understanding of how to move beyond it (not to be confused with the myth of making it go away) by accepting that it is there. It is then that we can honor it without getting mired in it, listen to it, understand it, check the facts, and work with it. It is hard to do. But that is true power.

About Shame

Eating Disorder Thought: "You are stupid, fat, worthless, and ugly. You don't deserve to be loved and no one would love someone as disgusting as you anyway."
Truth: So many of my clients have said some version of the above statement that it immediately pops into my brain when I think of lies eating disorders tell. My clients cannot imagine that others with eating disorders think similarly about themselves, because it is not true. How could this be true if you have loved ones in your life? It is an eating disorder trick—exception to the rule.

In over two decades of treating individuals suffering with eating disorders, I cannot remember meeting one who does not suffer from shame. I have heard shame researcher Brené Brown on numerous occasions say that shame is the fear that we are flawed and defective and therefore unworthy of love and connection. Shame plays a big role in the development of an eating disorder. Then shame plays a huge role in perpetuating an eating disorder. It gets to the point where my clients think that everything bad that happens is because they are bad. I challenge the lie by saying something out loud when anything bad happens, like a light bulb going out in my office: "Oh no. That light bulb just went out because you're stupid, fat, worthless, and ugly." Sounds weird put that way, doesn't it? Think about it, though. You do the same thing in your own mind. I just go public with it.

You may feel pride in discipline, willpower, self-control, being "better than," being clever, or having an identity. You may then feel shame for feeling pride. You may feel shame when you notice happiness, thinking you don't deserve it. You may feel shame for the conflict, lying, pulling away from or pushing away loved ones, loss of control, "weakness," kneeling in front of toilets, or desperation. You may judge yourself or others as "fat and gross," then feel ashamed of yourself for being "superficial." When you chronically feel shame, you isolate, disconnect, and feel unworthy. You might seek comfort in things like bingeing, and then feel shame in violating what the eating disorder insists will make you "thin and beautiful." You may find numbness in not eating or pride in spending calories. But you are lying to those around you in order to do it. Shame increases. This twisted merry-go-round makes me dizzy.

Shame can lead you to withdraw from those who can help you, or with whom you can feel the connection needed for a meaningful relationship and a hopeful and purposeful life, as feelings of unworthiness about your core nature and self-disgust run rampant. Then you might do things like insist on perfection from yourself or others, pretend you are perfect, please others, or push away and judge others in the attempt to protect yourself from being judged by them first. These things make eating disorders worse, as they further isolate you and convince you that you are unworthy of love and connection with others.

Shame probably made it harder to write your response to the last tool. Shame may have gotten you to skip the tool altogether. If the shame is getting in the way of something helpful, notice this. To help you learn to manage unnecessary shame, as well as eating disorder thoughts and urges, use this skill to fight back. For example, to decrease shame, go back and wholeheartedly respond to the tool anyway. Shame will make it terrifying to share your responses with a safe, caring person in your life. To decrease shame, identify that person and share with them anyway. It is the only way out of the tar pit of shame. This is how you start uncovering your authentic power.

Learn about emotions, understand them, and work with them skillfully and effectively. That you can stop or exterminate them with eating disorder behavior, a body that looks a certain way, or any other attempts to push them down, overpower them, or annihilate them is an illusion—it is not power. Instead of spending all of your strength "controlling" emotions because of fear that you will drown in them, you will eventually find authentic power in acknowledging them and doing what is necessary to navigate those you like and those you don't as just another part of life's journey. I call it going with the flow.

An open heart has me singing silently.
A closed one has me screaming out loud.

A secret buried in fear is fatal to the recovery process.
Open up your heart to others you trust today.
Share your secret anyway, and watch your recovery grow.
—Robyn

9.

Who the Hell Am I, Anyway?

Pizza Nights and Designer Handbags

By Robyn

The never enough-ness inside me drove my every move. I was as good as the last puff of smoke my friends and family blew up my ass and as bad as the last story I invented about a stranger's sideways glance. I sought everyone's approval, sometimes openly, sometimes covertly. It was not the job of those who loved me to validate and keep me at ease, but I'd understand if they said it felt to them like it was. I was the one who had to provide the self-esteem by taking different actions to build it. If I did not do this, I would have no choice but to look for it elsewhere. And *elsewhere* always led me back to the eating disorder or other self-destructive coping strategies.

The unshakable feeling that I needed to hustle to have others notice and approve of me was what drove me throughout my life. Once I began to question who I was, what my desires were, and what I wanted to bring to this world, it was the starting point to finding real joy and acceptance of self.

When I was thirteen, I started attending a weekend class for singing, jazz, tap, and drama. It lasted four hours per Saturday. I remember walking up the long set of worn, wooden stairs to the studio where the class was held. I paused on the landing to ask myself, "Who am I going to be today?" Because being me wasn't enough; in order to be okay in my own skin and not spend four hours comparing myself to the other child-star wannabes, I needed to strap on my armor before I hit the foyer. That's where they would be sitting, unavoidable, putting on their tap shoes, singing their practiced lyrics, or stretching for jazz class with Ms. Georgia.

It was not that these highly talented kids planned on making fun of me or talking behind my back. I'm sure at some point they did these things; I mean, what kid doesn't? Nevertheless, I have no idea how they felt about me for the most part. But try telling a kid with an eating disorder that. I've since learned to be the most wary of the stories I tell myself.

In my mind I invented judgmental dialogue my peers were saying about me whenever I was belittling myself for not reading Shakespeare correctly during a cold read or not being able to hit a note in a Whitney Houston song in music practice. Both, I may add, are almost impossible to do! I was comparing myself to them constantly—my body, my face, my talent, their wealth—wishing I were them. None of it was true. All of it was in my mind and was created, I think, to keep me focused on meaningless things rather than the deep fear that my world would fall apart in the shape of my mum and her illness. In the spirit of transparency and not attempting to gild the dung of emotions that hit us in early recovery, sometimes I still have to be mindful of this today. Anxiety, after all, is beneath it all.

I have learned that the true value of recovery is in the process of "checking in" with myself and honoring that voice (not the eating disorder, the other one) that longs to be heard and that encourages me to keep moving forward. With each positive action I take toward this, I secure more self-worth and self-compassion from deep within.

After I got over the initial shock in recovery that I had no idea who I was (I truly had absolutely no idea) and what I liked or disliked outside of the eating disorder behaviors, I started to turn it into a game. Sometimes I would try new things and watch how I felt when I was doing them to see if I liked them or not.

I found out that I enjoy the rush of flying through the sky hooked to a cable. I love really hot showers, singing out loud, making people laugh, kissing, hiking in the sun with a friend, sleeping, and being heard—witnessed. These are all vital to my spirit and purpose. I learned I am a social being, but love to curl up by myself with a book or Hulu after 9:30 p.m. I learned that I like deep conversation, and that idle chitchat like, "So what do you do for a living?" bores me.

I have learned that I am not my bank account or my car model, and my worth will never be threatened because of it. I've also learned that it's okay to want a nice car, have savings, and enjoy nice things. I am a human being who has made bad choices, but I am not a bad person because of them. I have learned that I am responsible for my behavior and my thoughts, and that calling for time out when I do not feel comfortable is true self-care. I believe that clarity comes in a pause, and with that clarity comes a sense of showing up for myself to honor what is trying to call out to me.

I have also learned that just because I know the right way to behave doesn't mean I will always choose the right action. Sometimes I get angry when I am in fear, exhausted, or hungry. I say things I wish I hadn't, don't exercise when my body is begging me to, and say yes when I want to say no. But I'm getting so much better at it, and so will you.

This is life, and I am learning. Always learning. I am far from perfect and far from fairytale fantastic. But I am learning to accept my faults with a little more compassion because, and I always come back to this, *I am human*. But really, it's because I want to. Having acceptance for where I am in the moment doesn't mean that I am excusing inappropriate behavior or not taking responsibility. It means I don't have to go into a panic attack about how horrible I am.

I now understand that even when I feel like I can't get through an emotional loss, by going through it, important things will be revealed, and that the way to get through it is to simply show up and breathe. I have also learned that I need something outside of myself to help me hand over my deep desire to control. I call this the Universal Energy. I have found great power in honoring the part in me that pulls from faith. I have learned that being a good mother is important to me, but is not defined by what school my children attend and what clothing brands I buy them. It is defined by the way I show up for them emotionally and how I provide safe boundaries for them to explore their own emotions without trying to save them. Most of the time hearing them out and letting them know that I see them (not a quick-glance-from-the-computer, but a focus-my-eyeballs-upon-them) is often all they need. Usually all I need to get out of my head is to have a real moment with my daughters. Connection and family matter to me.

I have learned that my ego (that part of me that needs to be right and the best at all times) is not always my amigo, but that having pride in what I do (that sense of accomplishment in knowing I've done my best) is a wonderful gift to give myself. I have learned that fitting in with others is passé and overrated, that my true friends accept me for who I am, warts and all. For me, friendships are what make this world go 'round. The true connections I experience on my (too infrequent) pizza nights with Andi, Nicole, and Emily are like fuel to my soul.

I have learned that designer handbags do not define my true character or worth, but they sure are pretty to look at. I have learned that changing careers does not make the old one a failure or a waste. I have also learned that missing a career that you dreamed about your entire life is hard. But in recovery, I get to create a career that incorporates all my passions and aligns them with my purpose—or even go back to old ones if I want—because truly, anything is possible if you're willing to put it out there. Change is inevitable in this life, and befriending it removes the need for regrets or "what ifs."

I have learned that when I get quiet and stop trying to force the issue, I can make decisions that best honor me, and in turn, honor all those around me. When I stopped in my tracks and said, "This is who I am; this is my story," I could begin to change and become the woman I had longed to become.

I gained trust in myself, and in turn, my body, as I began to allow myself food within a structure that created freedom. Within a short year of brutal honesty with myself, and eating within the safety net of the Structured Approach, I noticed a decreased attachment to my wanting to be perfect that was also mirrored in my food choices. My choices were dictated by my body's need, not the needs of the eating disorder. I learned that the moment I tried to interject my thoughts about food into my body's signals it was bound to throw it into a tizzy, so I don't do that anymore . . . most of the time.

My story was also being revealed within my food. I began to hate being confined to all the foods I once considered safe. Instead, over time, I began to love experimenting with foods and found my power in choices that once tipped me over the edge and into the *f*ck it* button of a binge. I came to loathe anything that associated itself with the diet mentality, such as calorie counting and weighing and measuring foods. All of it now made me feel trapped. I loved variety. My food choices began to mirror the way I wanted to live my life, fully and freely.

Food no longer plagued me as it once did, simply because it no longer held power. I also noticed that I no longer had the desire to binge or starve because I'd gained wisdom, experience, and truth through my structured eating. I also replaced the connection with food for true connection with people. I was no longer afraid of my food choices. I knew through my experience with the Structured Approach that weight gain was due to eating when I was not hungry or past being full and not as intricately gauged by the choices I made.

I found that the choices I made were now in direct proportion to how much fuel I needed and whether I actually liked the food I was eating. I was also at ease with dining out. In fact, that was one of my favorite things to do. I was more comfortable listening to what my body wanted to eat, and noticed that it was from that voice that I usually made my food decisions. My body had organically moved into a Mindful Approach; and this time, it was my mind that followed. I had turned a corner in my recovery.

The Mindful Approach was an organic process that I had been naturally practicing within the Structured Approach for many months. I wrestled a little with letting go of the structure, but I reminded myself that I could always go back to it if I felt, at any stage, unsafe. There is a magical freedom around food within the Mindful Approach. The obsession has long since been lifted, and the trust in myself and in my choices took the eating disorder's place.

I had long since noticed that I hadn't fluctuated dramatically in weight, or in my emotional state, like I had when I was in the disorder. Without a binge, there was no substantial weight gain, and all the extra pounds that belonged to the binges had disappeared. I was now at a weight that no amount of dieting in the past had ever sustained. My body chose the weight it would be, not me. I would be lying if I told you that the size of my body has never bothered me in my recovery though. Sometimes I still have a weight-conscious thought, usually during a time in my life where I feel like I don't have control, a time of great stress, and/or a bout of anxiety. Noticing signs of aging has also done it to me. But when this occurs, it is more like a little buzzing in my ear that I can shoo away than a sledgehammer to my brain. If at any time it does feel like a sledgehammer, I take that as an indication that there is something bothering me emotionally that needs to be addressed.

My food choices became about aligning to my truth and strength, and the woman I want to become who is free from body and food obsession—for the most part. My plate now tells a very different story from what it did with the eating disorder.

Evelyn Tribole, author of *Intuitive Eating* says, "When we become intuitive about eating, we become intuitive about life." It's true, dear readers. It's *really* true!

Pizza, Handbags, and Beyond

By Espra

Get Quiet

Eating Disorder Thought: Blah, blah, blah . . .

Truth: The eating disorder says nothing new. It just shows up. It is predictable, belligerent, and won't shut up long enough to let you hear yourself think.

Deep honesty with yourself and trusted others continues to be a crucial part of your recovery. The eating disorder's relentless harassment and mandates are possibly all you have been able to hear and think about for quite some time. Trying "not to think about it" works about as well as that old game where you "try not to think about pink elephants" for one minute. It can't be done. Obeying the disorder's mandates rewards you with a brief moment of peace from its constant reminders about your defectiveness and flaws. It has become your life. The eating disorder might now even be your identity.

Recovery involves finding ways, other than obeying the disorder, to slow down that eating disorder voice. It starts with creating one fleeting moment at a time of silencing the voice, decreasing its volume, or returning your attention to where you decide to put it. The unique current of your recovery will determine how quickly this shift happens. Research shows that a consistent practice of choosing where you place your attention, noticing when it has wandered, and bringing it back to the intended object of your focus helps you cultivate the skill to refocus and quiet unwanted thoughts and urges. This is called mindfulness practice, and when practiced regularly, it can increase your ability to pay attention for longer periods of time, regulate emotions, and increase kindness to yourself and others. There are about twenty additional beneficial changes to the brain from regular mindfulness practice. I suggest you track down some books, audio, website resources, or apps on this topic and get going. I often use the Headspace phone app. Other people like the Calm app. It doesn't have to be a big deal, and there are many fun ways to practice. Mindfulness practice also opens the door to being able to practice the mindful eating that is crucial for knowing when you are hungry, what you are hungry for, when you are full, discerning between emotional and physical hunger, etc. A client recently reported, "I'm not satiated after a binge. I just have a stomach that feels full, and I am full of shame."

As you cultivate your ability to focus your mind, it begins to get quiet. Like Robyn found, the pauses make way for clearer thinking that helps you hear the voice of your own wisdom and intuitive knowing, and then separates it from the eating disorder voice. That is how we all wake up, listen, and start to honor our authentic selves. It happens as you take one glimpse at a time into the frightening and peaceful stillness in between and beyond your habitual thoughts. The longer the pauses, the more you can see—in the words of a friend of mine, "That which brings a different possibility of the knowing of the self."

Check In with Yourself
Eating Disorder Thought: "Ha. Funny. What self? There's nothing there to check in with. That's why you have me. You are nothing."
Truth: When your thoughts, emotions, goals, and identity are wrapped around an eating disorder there's no way to figure out what could be there.

The eating disorder tells you it is the only place for you to get honest feedback about your shortcomings. It convinces you that by controlling food or the size of your body, you will measure up. Pay attention. You need to be brutally honest with yourself about your goodness. My clients say, "Argh! Espra, you just don't quit, do you?" I reply, "No. This is life or death, and I will always fight for your life." To catch the eating disorder lying about your goodness, watch for those all-or-nothing thoughts. Maybe you are beginning to recognize them as red flags that the eating disorder is directing your thoughts. Catch it in the act of convincing you that you are all bad or unworthy. Really? Is it actually possible for anyone to be either all (as in 100 percent) bad or all good? Yeah, yeah, you are an exception to the rule. I hope you have a fleeting thought that questions this lie as well.

Our brains are made with what I have heard Rick Hanson, PhD, psychologist and senior fellow of the Greater Good Science Center at UC Berkeley, say is "Velcro for the negative and Teflon for the positive." In survival situations this is useful, but otherwise it can be miserable. It is frustrating that the authentic voice of encouragement, wisdom, and intuition slips quietly away, and the eating disorder voice shouts its demands at full volume then sticks in the brain. It takes awareness and practice (mindfulness) to tune in to the authentic voice. Each time you attend to the voice of your authentic self, it is like watering a plant. It will eventually take root, and you will start to see and appreciate it as it makes its way through the soil and manure and heads for the light. Then you can begin to align your behavior with that voice, moving closer to the peace we find when we look within for fulfillment instead of looking outside ourselves.

Look carefully for thoughts or ideas that feel true and real to you, and watch out for those you think you are "supposed" to have, those you "shouldn't have," those that scare you, those that you think you cannot achieve, those you think you don't deserve. You will need to carefully consider your values, your likes, your dislikes—everything that you believe in. Robyn found a helpful way to do that by checking in with her body.

> Try this: Think of one thing that you know you like, perhaps a color. Then think of a color you know you don't like. Now look at each color for a while and notice the sensations in your body. Sensations give you cues about your true likes and dislikes.

Start to Consider Tier Two of the Three-Tier Approach:
The Mindful Approach to Eating

Eating Disorder Thought: "Skip this section. You already know when you are hungry and full."

Truth: Your eating disorder thoughts tell you when you are hungry and full. Think about its agenda. You can't trust the eating disorder's information if you are going to recover from it. However, your body is not an accurate informant for nutrition right now either. It is off balance, out of practice, and generally confused about hunger and its nutritional needs.

If you want to consider alternatives to being the prisoner of an eating disorder, you will need to get honest about the things you may find the most terrifying to face—food and eating. Getting honest about when you are physically hungry and when you are physically full loosens the control of the eating disorder over you. Robyn calls this "listening to your body's mind." It is the antithesis of listening to the eating disorder's mandates or using food in the attempt to manage emotions. You must become aware of and override prior learning—rules about "good" or "bad" foods, amounts, when and why to start eating and stop eating. Even if you are reading this book and do not have an eating disorder, some of the thoughts and emotions that lead you to eat or not eat might surprise you: "It's been a hard day. I am tired and stressed. I deserve some ice cream." Or "It's been a hard day. Forget eating. I deserve a vacation from having to think about food or eating for the rest of the day."

It took Robyn about a year of using the Structured Approach to eating before she was able to maintain her own safety around food and trust her body enough to allow it to guide her eating, despite her thoughts, rules, or fears. Consider the time you spend with the Structured Approach like learning to walk a tightrope. It provides an anchor to train your balance, with a safety net beneath you. You gain trust in yourself, your choices, and your body based on the skills you are using, rather than the deceptions of your eating disorder. It takes time to stabilize your body physically, to increase your capacity for thinking logically about alternatives, as well as to stabilize preoccupation with food. It takes time to stabilize your fears about eating, what food will do to you, "losing control," and feeling satiated. It takes time to restore your metabolism, your body's optimal functioning, and a more balanced lifestyle in general. It takes time to restore your body's ability to register nutritional information and give signals to your brain based on that. If you try to move beyond the Structured Approach before all of these things are more stable, it will fail. You can find yourself restricting nutrition or bingeing because your body is not yet stable and skilled enough to use its own wisdom in a way that supports recovery.

> **Getting honest about when you are physically hungry and when you are physically full loosens the control of the eating disorder over you.**

Recovery cannot be rushed, as the price of falling without a safety net is high. Robyn and I feel that a minimum of one year with the Structured Approach makes sense. Determine with your dietitian how long you need to use a structured eating plan before you have the skills to meet the challenge of a more flexible plan.

Only then will the Mindful Approach to eating benefit you. The Mindful Approach has structure, but less than the Structured Approach. You will begin to choose what, when, and how much to eat, surrounded by the safety net of eating regular meals and snacks to meet your body's physical and chemical needs. If you are not hungry at all, regardless of the reason, it is still important to keep some structured intake, but you may choose to eat less than when you are hungry.

In the past few years more resources have become available to help you learn ways to practice eating mindfully. An amazing resource to help you better understand what mindful eating entails as well as tools for approaching it is the groundbreaking book, *Intuitive Eating* by Evelyn Tribole, RD and Elyse Resch, RD. Education and your own registered dietitian are the best resources to help you supplement your information for this phase of your recovery.

The Mindful Approach is about paying careful attention to your emotions, hunger, cravings, the flavors of food, how your experience changes as you eat, and when food becomes less enjoyable to your taste buds, instead of paying attention to your thoughts and emotions. You move away from ideas of "good" and "bad" foods and let your body choose a wide variety of foods that sound good, rather than a narrow range of "safe" foods and amounts. Consider additional personal variables as well. For example, some medications can block the brain's ability to register when it is time to eat or when you have had enough to eat. To mindfully eat, you may have to monitor the physical sensations of pressure and fullness in your stomach to indicate when you are full because your brain won't tell you when you've had enough to eat.

 To prepare for the Mindful Approach, identify your (versus the eating disorder's) food likes and dislikes. Identify every thought, rule, feeling, belief, and habit that has a part in your relationship with food beyond physical hunger or fullness. Make a detailed list of

these things that direct your choices about when or when not to eat, what to eat or not eat, and how much. Be specific. Then go back through your list several times to add things you initially missed.

Example: 1) I am stressed out. I want to relax with my favorite ice cream. I choose the flavor and amount based on my desire to relax with ice cream instead of sensations in my belly or on my taste buds. 2) I feel stressed and anxious; I don't want to hassle with choosing, preparing, or eating food, so I don't eat. 3) If I eat more than others, I am a pig, so I make sure I eat less than them, regardless of how hungry I am or when I last ate. I may even go home and binge after. 4) If my stomach is growling and it's mid-morning, I can't eat because it's not yet noon. So I have more coffee. 5) I love fresh bread. I have to eat all I can before it is gone. I start my diet again on Monday. 6) It is wasteful not to eat everything on my plate.

No one perfects mindful eating. Sometimes you will become overly hungry or overly full. Eating unmindfully in one instance does not equate to failing at mindful eating; it is human because it is an ongoing "practice." We wake up, notice that we are not mindfully eating, and then return to the Mindful Approach as soon as possible. It is a lifetime process. We remember that each moment is a brand-new chance to make a different choice. Sometimes we notice, yet we don't want to do it differently. This is an opportunity to take a look at what emotion, thought, or belief might be driving the behavior and consider our options. The Mindful Approach is made up of a set of skills that we must strive to continually develop and honor with practice and time. It cannot be perfected. It is difficult. It is liberating.

Deserving and Worth
Eating Disorder Thought: "You don't deserve to eat. You don't deserve to enjoy food. You don't deserve to recover. You don't deserve to be happy."
Truth: This is how eating disorders operate for most people. As you've read, Robyn's drove her to go to extraordinary lengths to earn the approval of others.

They come at you with a vengeance, like arrows at a target. They pierce your mind and your heart, driving into you that you are nothing without an eating disorder, nothing but an invisible "other" or someone who takes up too much space in a crowd, and deserve nothing more. They convince you that you will never stand out as unique, interesting, or appealing because there is nothing special about you. You don't deserve to eat; you don't deserve to stop eating; you don't deserve to be free of punishment (even if you have to continue it yourself with the help of your humble servant, the eating disorder). Catch these lies!

My clients are certain they are the only ones in the world who feel inadequate, unworthy, or unlovable. They are not. Robyn was not, and you are not. Keep paying skeptical attention to that eating disorder voice. As you try to pull away, it will bounce back. Keep talking back to it. It doesn't have to be your identity. Right now you are starting to piece together your own identity aside from the eating disorder, and we are helping you get started.

Do you live in fear that unless you are perfect, someone will see through your facade, exposing the truth that you are a fraud, an empty shell? Are you convinced that most people judge you negatively and see you as "less than," even if they won't admit it? Does it seem like you were born defective, but can't put your finger on exactly how? Does any of this sound familiar? It is the shame that convinces you that you are flawed and defective, therefore unworthy of love and connection. The eating disorder loves this stuff. If I were filled with a cold, dark, consuming certainty that I was defective, I wonder if I might go to any lengths, maybe even self-destructive ones, to get away from it as well.

Most everyone feels varying degrees of this. You read it right. I know, I know . . . the difference is that *they* aren't defective and *you* are. Busted, eating disorder! It is using an exception to the rule. You are special only in a negative way, or so it tells you. It is so common for people to fear being exposed as a fraud that it has a name: "Imposter Syndrome." For instance, I am convinced that people often think I am more competent and know more than I really do. If they knew the truth about what I do and do not know, they would know I'm a fraud. People might tell me otherwise, but they are just being nice. Robyn has confided in me that she has the same feelings. But how can Robyn be silly enough to think that about herself? She is amazing.

Use this information to question the eating disorder. Ask around, check the facts, consider the evidence, and use those to draw a logical conclusion instead of relying on the stories in your head.

Feeling unworthy can lead to extreme efforts to be perfect as a way to earn value and worth. The problem is that imperfection is the human condition. Human beings are bound to break any streak of perfection because that's how we (you included) are made. The eating disorder says you must rise above human imperfection in order to be good enough. This comes at a great cost to you, your time, your relationships, and your life. Is the picture of the craziness of eating disorder expectations getting any clearer?

Even when you get a fleeting sense of being worthwhile as a result of being the "best" at restricting your nutrition, spending unwanted calories, eating "healthy," being the perfect size or weight, it is temporary. That is the transient nature of using outside measures to define your worth or value. It is like winning the big prize at a carnival game. You are good, you are the best, and everyone can see it. Then you see someone with the same prize. You are deflated. The feelings of inadequacy rise up, and you feel compelled to go back, spend your money, and be the best again. I have heard Brené Brown say, "Comparison is the thief of happiness." The real question here is how much satisfaction do you get from having a life-sized stuffed panda in your room at home? And how long will that satisfaction last?

Human beings are bound to break any streak of perfection because that's how we (you included) are made.

Figuring Out What Makes You Tick

Eating Disorder Thought: "Look, just get everything else done first and then you'll have time to sit around and think about anything you want."

As you get quiet and honestly consider your essence, you begin to get glimpses of your interests, talents, and strengths. You haven't had the mental space to attend to such matters thanks to the eating disorder's chatter and illusions. First things first: The best way to run back to your eating disorder for security and comfort is to believe that your only choices are the extremes of figuring out who you are all at once or living in isolation behind your painful mask of "safety" with your eating disorder.

Question these illusions; that's what recovery is made of. That's what life is made of. I have a sign in my office that says, "We do not *find* who we are, we *create* who we are." Figuring out who you are is a lifelong, ongoing process. For Robyn, beginning to question her desires and deciding what she wanted to bring to the world was a part of her early path to finding herself and true peace. Robyn wasn't *finding* self-esteem; she was *creating* it based on her authentic desires, passions, values, and goals, by creating day-to-day actions that lined up with those desires, passions, values, and goals. You likely have either lost these parts of yourself or never known them at all. Expect to feel terrified that there is no "self" to be found. Try to focus instead on how to build yourself up. Self-esteem is built from each positive action that supports a part of your authentic self. Each action that you take toward supporting those parts of your authentic self builds your foundation by securing your self-esteem from deep within. Along the way, work to speak to yourself like you would speak to someone you love, as I have heard self-compassion researcher Kristin Neff, PhD repeatedly say.

Make a list of sixty-seven things that you think you might like to see, learn, or do before you die. Include everything . . . big, small, seemingly out of reach. If you run out of things to put on your list, which you will, add smaller steps toward some items and add "stupid little things." Choose one item from your list that you want to pursue first. List all of the steps you would have to take to make that particular goal real for you. If you feel overwhelmed after listing the steps, go back and insert smaller steps between the larger ones. Keep breaking down each step until it feels doable. All steps are possible when you break them down enough. Make sure the goal is your own, and make the steps toward your goal enjoyable and interesting to you. Sixty-seven lines are a lot to fill. Stay with it; keep coming back to it and get through it any way you can. It need not and cannot be "perfect" or "right." It just has to stimulate your brain to consider the possibilities. I promise, neither Robyn nor I will hold you to any single thing you write on this list. If you are going to create a life outside of your eating disorder, you absolutely need a list!

Example: 1) Stay at New York, New York casino in Las Vegas. 2) See a favorite singer live in concert. Steps: Look up their concert schedule, see the cost of tickets, find a way to save that amount of money, purchase a ticket, get to the concert.

If you notice yourself thinking that some of the items on your list are "stupid," too big, too small, unattainable, unacceptable, not feminine or masculine enough, against the wishes of someone else, wishful thinking—write them down anyway. It is the only way to tap into your authentic desires. Some will go against what others want for you, what they think is okay, or what you "should" want or do. There will be others that you believe you want because you are "supposed" to want them. Write those down also. This is the kind of honesty I am talking about. It is hard to write down what you think you like or want when you have no earthly idea what these things might be. Warning: No eating disorder goals allowed.

Most of us have heard stories about people getting inspired to run out and do all of the things they've always wanted to do before they died. You are in the opposite situation. It is as if you have been dead, at least inside, and you are now hustling to think of everything you always wanted to do when you woke up. This act will wake you up. This will begin to develop in you an authentic sense of self, identity, and worth.

Ruling Out What Doesn't Make You Tick
Eating Disorder Thought: "Go ahead. Make their stupid list. Just write things . . . anything. It doesn't matter. You are hollow, shallow, and so dull that there's nothing to find no matter how many things you write on a piece of paper."
Truth: Yes, go ahead and write just anything. Figuring out who you are is done by experimenting with many things to learn both what you like and what you don't like.

For once, let's just go along with those eating disorder thoughts. You jumped through the hoop and made your list just to say that you made a list. What happens if you set out to experiment with items on it and have to scratch them off because you find you don't like them or they are things that someone else wanted you to dream? To find answers to the "Who the hell am I, anyway?" question, you will need to experiment with the things on your list, getting a sense for what you like and want to explore further versus what you don't like. It can be as fun to scratch items off your list as it is to discover what you want to continue to pursue. Right here, right now as you are considering this, you are learning who you are, partly through learning who you are *not*. And that's the way it's done. My "Life Goals" list (posted in my planner so I can always keep them in mind) once had skydiving on it. I would HATE skydiving. I'm more of the riverboat ride at Disneyland kind of girl.

It can be helpful to say the eating disorder's answers to the "Who the hell am I?" question out loud. I'd suggest doing so somewhere private, since you will be talking to yourself. "Who the hell am I?"

"I am an eating disorder. That's who I am."

"Who am I?" "I am a fat, lazy slob who can't stop eating."

"Who am I?" "I am the one with enough self-discipline to eat salad with no cheese or dressing (and talented enough at acting to convince others that I like it that way)."

"Who am I?" "I am clever enough to devise a million reasons to skip a meal."

"Who am I?" "I am the math wizard who calculates how many calories I've ingested and how much exercise it takes to burn them (plus a little more)."

"Who am I?" "I am just a number."

Say these answers aloud and really listen to them. In the words of a past client, "Congratulations, I am the very best at something that matters the very least in life."

Check Your Ego at the Door

Eating Disorder Thought: "If you control what you eat well enough, you can finally be worthwhile and good enough for people to love and accept you."

Eating Disorder Thought: "You feel proud? That's conceited. You should be ashamed of yourself for being so haughty and prideful. The only time you can feel proud is when you are perfect at doing what I tell you to do."

Truth: I'm calling "twisted logic, eating disorder," on this one. Remember the disorder's love for using two sides of the same coin to argue its point? When you catch it in the process, it can tip you off that it's out to win, no matter what, and that, in the words of a past client, "ED's messing with your head."

My clients struggle with the idea of pride, often believing that it is egotistical and wrong. Some of us are taught this. Depending on where you look to find a definition of pride, it can look like either a desirable or an undesirable character trait. However, when you live in a way that aligns with your long-term goals and values, a sense of self-acceptance and inner peace starts to take root. It is different from the pride you experience when others or the eating disorder give you approval. This pride moves you toward a sense of self-respect, self-esteem, or satisfaction because of what you are doing. Then it moves into pride about who you are, and, although it will feel strange, there is nothing wrong with that kind of pride.

Stop Trying to Fit in

Eating Disorder Thought: "Duh. If you weren't such a misfit, others would accept you, and you wouldn't have so work so hard to fit in. But you are. So you do."
Truth: People lose interest when you describe your most exciting endeavor as having the "self-discipline" to resist donuts, or lack of willpower to resist them or get rid of the calories after eating them. What the eating disorder ignores is that you have nothing interesting to say about your life, what you are doing, your dreams or goals because the eating disorder is your life, and the eating disorder is boring!

What if you had an alternative? What if you began to identify and create experiences around your goals and interests, rather than around which foods you resisted or consumed, efforts to control your body, or what you think others want you to be? What if you looked around in your world, found, and surrounded yourself with others who have similar likes, interests, goals, and values? You just might feel some acceptance, and acceptance is more enduring than approval. Perhaps this approach might seem to bring things other than misery to your life.

Start tuning in to hear the whispers of your internal voice. Expect there to be fear that only a worthless core or empty shell will be exposed when you try this new type of focus. Then tune in to it anyway. Remember the time and energy you have invested in an effort to hide your core being. It takes your eating disorder to cover it up. And it makes you miserable. A mentor of mine says eating disorder thinking says, "Who do I need to be for you to approve of me?" Recovery thinking says, "This is who I am. I hope you are okay with that." This begins the life-long journey of discovering who you are.

The ride is much more fun when you let go.

There are times when we feel like we are hanging on to anything that will hold us up and safeguard us from the rollercoaster of life and its emotions— like our diet, our body size, and the story we tell others. But the truth is, life is a journey, and there is no safeguarding ourselves from anything.

Today I will let go of fear. I will let go of the expectation that the eating disorder can and will safeguard me from being hurt. I will embrace the unknown and let go, enjoying the ride of life.

—Robyn

10.

Speak Out. Speak Your Truth. Speak Strong!

Gushing Rivers and Shocking Phone Calls

By Robyn

Fear of my secrets dissolved the more I spoke them. The more I spoke them, the more they lost their power. The more I witnessed the lack of their power, the more my sense of self grew. This is what ultimately replaced the cycle of the eating disorder.

One of the most challenging things about recovery was learning how I really felt about things. I was so used to trying to please others, or delegating the responsibility to other people to make decisions, that I had lost connection and trust with my own truth. Often I would find myself just nodding my head when someone in a social situation would say something, or not commenting on something I felt passionate about on social media because I was scared of offending someone—or worse—I got it wrong. I feared looking and feeling stupid. Within most conversations where strong opinions were involved and others seemed adamant about what they were saying, I figured they were right, and nodding or not writing what I felt prevented me from having to partake in the conversation. I got by for many years on my acting skills.

With my loved ones, I often spoke from both sides of my mouth. I would find myself becoming angry if Tim wanted to comment about something I said. I took his need to comment as a challenge to catch me out. The statements he questioned were made up of disjointed resentments, fears, and judgments that had built up each time I had not put a voice to them. They ran out of my mouth like water that had been blocked by a boulder gushing from a river—sometimes raging and damaging. When the boulder is removed, the force and speed causes the river flow to be powerful and choppy, just like the combination of my thoughts and emotions. My practice of saying nothing in order to get through uncomfortable conversations without causing waves was now causing floods.

Often in our household, I said things I thought Tim wanted to hear. I wanted him to love me, approve of me, and want to be with me. Because of this habit, there was no honoring of my truth and I had no self-worth as a result. I couldn't understand why he wanted to question things that I had only said because I thought he wanted to hear them. Was it because I didn't believe what I was saying, so neither did he? I believe now that Tim didn't believe me because I didn't believe me. But in order to change that, I needed to speak from my truth so that truth could form a solid foundation for our relationship. But speaking my truth frightened me.

I'd go to any lengths not to be disliked. My insides squirmed whenever I was confronted with the possibilities. I'd scramble like a hamster the moment I was called to own my value or honor my needs, especially if they conflicted with others' needs. I just wanted to make the problem better and move on as if nothing happened.

Everything we force down or to which we give no voice will come up. It must. It was the stuffing down and festering that caused more damage than speaking my truth ever could have. With all the resentment that surfaced during my recovery, I had to ask myself, "What have I done in my life that was so horrible that I cannot trust myself or my needs?" It felt like such a loaded, scary question.

It's a scientific fact that when our bodies go into flight or fight mode, our brains will scan our environment to find the immediate danger. If there is none, they will create a story. When our bodies are in a constant state of anxiety, our minds attempt to find the bogeyman from which they are running, and we tend to make that bogeyman us, rather than our anxiety. When we have made ourselves the bogeyman for so many years, it is difficult to trust ourselves. In recovery, we must review this and separate ourselves from it *over* and over again.

I have done nothing that the bogeyman tells me I have, except to place expectations on myself that I should know everything and be everything to everyone—oh, and have no needs. When I really sat with this outlandish expectation and asked myself if I would put the same expectation on anyone else, I almost laughed out loud at the absurdity of it all. I began to question what I was running from when I did not speak my truth. What did it provide me? I mean, there must be a pay-off, right? Even if it was to relieve myself of the squirminess I felt internally, or the sheer panic I felt whenever I thought I was the bogeyman. I was affecting my relationship with myself and my relationships with others. I had to address the anxiety that kept me quiet and fearful, and then ask myself what kind of relationships I was setting up for myself if they all were based on a character so far removed from who I really was.

The recognition of this truth gave me the power to begin speaking it. I wanted to experience who I was and be able to maintain recovery. I couldn't do that pretending to be someone else. Not only was it confusing and void of any real intimacy (let's face it, without truth there is no intimacy), but it also kept me wanting to seek the familiar in the eating disorder. I *couldn't* afford that.

◆ ◆ ◆

When I was in treatment for substance use and depression, an extended family member questioned my motives in having my girls come to visit me. He and his wife were minding our girls during the days while Tim was at work, and they were attempting to soothe our toddlers' hearts by telling them that I had gone on vacation to Australia to visit my family. Although I knew their comments to my girls came from a place of love, it was unacceptable to me that my children believed I went to Australia without them. The truth was their mommy was unwell, much like someone who has a physical ailment and needs it tended to. Their mommy, by going to treatment, was looking after herself so she could be a present mommy. A better mommy. I called my treatment "Mommy Camp." It was a camp that I needed to get through the trauma of losing my own Mummy, and to break the cycle of depression and learn how to self-soothe without using substances. Asking for and getting help not only helps us, but also all those around us. If it weren't for treatment, I would not be here writing this book today.

When it was time for my girls to visit me, the extended family member, who I believed to care for me and with whom I felt I had a fairly good relationship,

> **Asking for and getting help not only helps us, but also all those around us.**

contacted the treatment center directly to question the decision my therapist and I had agreed upon to have the girls visit. I believe now that his action was motivated by a desire to protect them emotionally, and in that he chose not to speak to Tim or me before doing so, and instead contacted a friend of a friend who worked at the treatment center where I was staying. In treatment facilities, staff members must have patients' written consent to even comment on whether patients are in the facility or not. Only Tim and my brother, Anton, were on the list of people who could discuss my treatment progress. Therefore, the staff could not respond to the concerns my extended family member raised. As a result, the staff informed my counselor, and in the next session, encouraged me to deal with the fact that my extended family member was questioning a decision the staff and I had come to, a decision that we knew to be in the best interest of my children, my husband, and myself.

Oh wow. Oh shit. I was encouraged to get on the phone and ask my extended family member if there was something I could tell him in response to his call. *How could I do this when my children were staying at his home with his wife? How could I, being someone in treatment, question him? How could I be both grateful and have boundaries?*

Thank God for the support of the two staff members sitting close by as I dialed the phone to him. I followed the script of my counselor, asking if I could help him with his questions. He didn't like it. He told me I was being selfish and that he had never liked me because we were "oceans apart." No happy ending there. But even then when his response was as evident as a bruise from a punch in the face, I questioned myself and my right to create boundaries.

If that wasn't bad enough, and in my opinion it was, in the next session with my counselor, we had a follow-up call with my extended family member. My counselor wanted to clarify his words from the first call, which I thought (hoped) I must have misinterpreted. But again, during a phone therapy session with my counselor, he stated that he "didn't care for me." Ouch. Squirm. I had to sit with this shocking information. It was *his* truth, and what our relationship was when the smoke and mirrors and the rising of resentment came up and made everything worse than if we had spoken our truths a long time ago. As shocking as it was to me (I really had no idea), it was liberating!

After that phone call and resulting therapy session, I began to sit with the truth that someone didn't like me, and I couldn't do anything about it. A truth that I thought was unbearable. And I survived it. Not only did I survive it, but in an odd way, I felt free. Truth be told, I was tired of trying so hard to be the perfect family member. For as much as I hated the squirmy feeling, I hated equally the feeling when I caught myself acting like a character I saw in a movie who I thought had it all together, rather than just being me and owning it.

The breakthrough with my extended family member is that I have boundaries in that relationship when it comes to topics of conversation in which I choose to participate now. Turns out we *are* oceans apart. And I'm okay with that. Some things I feel comfortable speaking to him about, and some things are uncomfortable, unnecessary, or even harmful for me to share. I no longer feel compelled to sacrifice my honesty and my self-respect by trying to control whether or not he approves of me; I no longer need his approval in order to feel okay about myself. What I do require is that he honors and respects the gift of being a part of my daughters' lives, and he truly does this with great love.

Here's another thing: No one had ever told me that "I don't know" was an acceptable answer to a question. Or even, "I'm not sure about that, can I get back to you?" I always had a sense that I had to respond in a flash. I had what I now like to call "self-imposed urgency." I believed that taking the time to think about my responses showed people that I had no idea about things. I was so busy trying to protect an image I thought others wanted to see and to which they would be attracted. They wanted to see "the woman behind the curtain," and instead I gave them "the almighty Oz."

I also thought shooting from the hip was quirky and admirable, but how I chose to use those traits was inappropriate and was only reflection of my fear and low self-worth. My job in recovery became about unlocking my truth, then speaking and acting from it. The fear of "What will happen if I do so?" diminishes with the reality of what actually happens when I have done so.

One Colorado spring day, the girls and I were having some afternoon tea. While serving them, I pretended to write down their orders with a "thank you, madams" and went to leave the table. Both girls stopped me with their "Mummy!"

"You forgot to take the menus." Lilly said.

"Yeah, Mummy. Waiters are supposed to take the menus from the tables." Chloe protested.

"Okay! Stop bossing me!" I joked.

Lilly's based-on-fact response: "I'm just teaching you how to be a waiter, because you don't know, Mummy." And although it was a joke, she was right. My unconscious perception that I need to know everything appears to be still alive. But at least, for the most part, its consequences are benign.

Today, I continue to learn that to withhold my truth is to withhold intimacy and connection. Yet truth begins with self. On this journey of recovery, facing my truth, my story, my life as it is—with all its confusion, shades of emotions, faults, passions, and humanity—is enough. When I speak my truth, I also give others the permission to speak theirs, just like my extended family members did.

These days, I do my best to take pride in my responses to others. I quiet the bogeyman within and ask myself, "Is it a snake or a stick?" Gosh, most often, it's a stick. Even during my public speaking, I have learned to pause in front of hundreds. You can hear me responding to questions by saying, "I don't know the answer to that. I'd love your details so I can get back to you when I have found someone who does." Ha! Who knew that the truth really *can* set us free?

How to Stand Still in a Current

By Espra

Unlock Your Truth

Eating Disorder Thought: "You're fat and undisciplined. That is your truth. I'm just telling you the truth because one else will."

Truth: This is not truth. This is name calling. This is verbal abuse. I hope no one in your life calls you names, and if they do, I hope you can get them to stop or get away from them.

As you practice listening beyond the eating disorder's lies to uncover your authentic desires, you develop the capacity to see yourself honestly. At this point, you will be well into your own recovery journey. You are unlocking your own truths. You start to look at who you really are, and gradually decrease your dependence on your eating disorder to define, hide, or perfect you. You challenge the urge to let your fear keep you mute. You begin to peel off parts of the eating disorder mask to slowly

> **Courage comes *after* we do what we are afraid to do.**

reveal what's behind it—your authentic thoughts, feelings, and preferences. And yes, you feel terror because you risk losing something that's been so important you would lay down your life for it—this disorder, which promised the approval of others so you could feel accepted, and thus worthwhile.

Living your truth takes courage. You won't trust it, yet. Keep doing it, and self-trust will begin to sneak up on you. Remember, courage comes *after* we do what we are afraid to do. This is how you will begin to trust yourself. It is the opposite of denying your feelings, hiding, and people-pleasing. A difficult truth is that you are not perfect, never will be, and no attempts to control your size, shape, or eating will make you so. And you are worthwhile, acceptable, and lovable anyway.

You know by now that eating disorders are driven by shame, and guilt loves to go along for the ride. Then, in turn, eating disorder behaviors like lying, deception, and violating your values increase the shame and guilt. The intertwined connection of each to the other takes you further down the slippery slope of misery. A large part of recovery is about decreasing the shame and isolation that both cause and are perpetuated by the hiding and dishonesty. Looking beyond the shame helps you see from all angles of honesty to help you block the eating disorder's hold on you. Otherwise, the disorder can block you by convincing you that you are being forthright and honest when it is only partially the case. Dishonesty can take multiple forms. To consider the full spectrum of your behavior, values, and beliefs about honesty, it is helpful to ask yourself whether or not your idea of honesty includes the following: answering a direct question truthfully; what you leave out or don't say; knowing that a person believes something that is not true or complete and allowing them to continue believing it anyway.

It helps to consider shame when you are considering the question of honesty with others. It is not best to set about being indiscriminately and totally honest with everyone. That can backfire, and the eating disorder will be thrilled to remind you that it was right. Getting honest with others begins with creating as much safety as possible. Begin to unlock your truth by preparing to discuss it with someone who is unlikely, based on concrete evidence, to reject you because of it. Of course you won't feel 100 percent safe as you embark on this task, so it is important to create as much structure and safety as possible to allow you every advantage.

 Consider the people in your life, such as therapists, parents, siblings, extended family, friends, leaders, clergy, and support groups. 1) Make a list of people to whom it might be safe to reveal parts of yourself. These are people with whom there is a lower risk of rejection. 2) For each person, write down the facts: What have you personally seen that person do or heard that person say that will provide evidence about whether or not he or she will hold information about you in a nonjudgmental and safe manner? Use this information to draw factual conclusions about those who might be the least likely to reject you based on what you disclose to them. Some will still kick you in the teeth if you take this risk, and you will begin to find authentic connection with others if you take this risk. We are made for connection.

For example, your aunt eats mindfully, never talks about dieting, forbidden foods, or disliking her body or others' bodies. Those facts logically suggest that she would be a safe person with whom to discuss your eating disorder. In contrast, you hear a friend repeating things others have told her in confidence. She would not be a safe person to confide in. Even if she says she will protect your truths, you see her actions and hear her speak otherwise. The risk is high that she will do the same with you. Again, make sure that the people you eliminate from consideration are rejected based on actual evidence, and not from your shame or fear.

Also, make sure you choose individuals who are not likely to reinforce your eating disorder thinking, who will not expect you to be perfect in order to be good enough, and who will hold you accountable for not staying honest.

Speak from Your Truth

Eating Disorder Thought: "Whatever. Go ahead and tell people everything about you, and watch what happens. You'll be sorry."

Truth: Extremes are a tool of the eating disorder. Honesty does not mean telling people everything, as that is just as dangerous as totally hiding your self, thoughts, and feelings.

Like Robyn, you will find that the power of your secrets and shame decreases as you speak of them where it is safe to do so. Gather concrete evidence about how many people jump up and run out of the room screaming because of what you reveal. Use the facts that you gather as ammunition against the eating disorder's lies. A crucial element of using behavior that is contrary to your shame is to do it "all the way." In DBT we teach clients how to guide their facial expressions, posture, and tone of voice, and speak up as if they have nothing to be ashamed of. You will be terrified. Do it anyway. This is how we build faith in ourselves that we can take risks.

Speaking your truth helps you take care of yourself and the relationships in your life. When we suppress our thoughts, feelings, needs, and wants, we build resentment and tension on both sides, and things blow up or fall apart. Telling others what is and is not okay with you in a kind way makes them feel safer, like you feeling safer when they do so with you. You will have to practice tolerating when others speak their truth in order to build these authentic relationships. Please gently consider that to not tell others what you need, think, or feel, or to act as if you are perfect, hiding your vulnerabilities and struggles, is deceptive.

Have you ever had a relationship with someone who is always doing great, who has no problems or needs? It's hard to feel close or connected to that person. Sometimes, not chronically, expressing sadness draws us closer to others. Otherwise, there is no way for others to know if they have hurt or offended you. They never get the chance to make things right. This lack of expression even makes me nervous in therapeutic relationships. I cannot know when clients are overwhelmed by an assignment unless they tell me. They may not tell me for fear of my disapproval or judgment. I may never know that I am making things worse for them. It is ultimately up to all of us to know for ourselves, and then let others know, what is and what is not in our best interest.

Being honest with others carries some responsibility. Be sure to speak your truth to others in ways that are consistent with your long-term values and how you want to treat others. I have had clients who have told me that I don't care about them, and they hate me. They told me that they were just trying to be honest like I asked them to. I can handle and work with that as a therapist. But it does tend to alienate others and get in our way if we want or need any sort of relationship with them. Honesty is not an excuse for being unkind. It is possible to be honest in gentle, kind, and compassionate ways.

Act from Your Truth

Eating Disorder Thought: "You made the wrong decision. If you had stayed in that job, you would be happy. Now you are miserable because you made a stupid decision. You're so stupid."

Truth: There is rarely such a thing as a perfect decision. Most decisions will have outcomes that we both like and dislike. We gather the facts, make the best decision we can, and get on with our lives. If the outcome is unacceptable, we make a decision to address that.

Though you are probably not ready to trust your decisions, it is important to keep practicing making the best ones you can, based on facts. The outcome of most decisions will have aspects that you both like and don't like. For instance, if you encounter a problem in a new job, you might not consider the possible negatives of having stayed at your old one. You might conclude that you would be happier, or at least less miserable, if you had not changed jobs. Do not use this feeling to beat yourself up for making a "bad" or "stupid" decision. Although it seems that criticizing ourselves will make us better in the future, research shows such change is only short-term. Our brain perceives it as a threat, catapults into survival mode, and hijacks our thoughts and emotions in a way that pulls us away from valued or goal-driven action. It makes us anxious and shut down. Most decisions are reversible to some degree. So practice making the best decisions you can with the information you have. Making decisions and learning from them is how we build the skill of making and learning to trust our decisions.

Another way to act from your truth is to back up verbal limits you set with others by knowing what you do or don't have control over, and acting within those limits. If you don't, you run the risk of feeling powerless, then running to your eating disorder and its illusions of control. That's exactly the place you are working so hard to stay away from. The next tool can help you find ways to set your limits with others and hold those limits with your actions, if necessary. Other people, often unaware of what is helpful or harmful in your journey toward recovery, may say and do things that leave you reeling and trigger intense eating disorder thoughts and feelings.

1) Make a list of triggering statements that others have said or might say. Examples: "I wish I could make myself throw up when I eat too much. I've tried but I can't." "Have you gained weight?" "You've lost some weight, you look good." "Just eat healthy food and don't buy junk food." "Just eat." 2) For each of these triggering words or phrases, write down what you might say, not say, do, or not do, when you hear them, then practice saying your responses out loud.

Examples:
 • **Sarcasm: "I can't tell you. It's classified information."**
 • **Radical Genuineness: "It's a brutal thing to go through. I**

wouldn't recommend it for anyone."
- Education: "When you say, 'You look healthy,' it brings my attention back to my body, and I need my attention to be on things like my traits, goals, and values."
- Statistics: "Diets don't work. Within five years, dieters gain back the weight they lost plus more."
- Fogging: "I'd prefer not to talk about that." (Continue same statement until they run out of steam.)
- Quick getaway: "Oh geez! I'm late. Gotta go!" (Briskly walk away.)

Always remember that just because someone asks you a question does not mean you are obligated to provide the information he or she is asking for. You have some control here. However, in the best interest of your recovery, it is to your advantage to teach those in your life what is helpful, not helpful, and harmful to say to you. Ultimately, it is up to us to coach others on how we need to be treated.

Use both your brain and your emotions. Use your voice. Take pride in uncovering your truths as you walk through this life. Hold your head high and speak your truth with conviction, kindness, and seriousness—even if you are scared. Live your truth. Bring your actions into alignment with your values and goals. This is the blueprint not only for the structure of recovery from your eating disorder, but for your dream home . . . a life that is worth living.

Everyone has a guide on the inside.
And its name is not "eating disorder."
Its name is "truth."

Today, I will embrace my authentic self. Who I really am and what I have to say is worth attention. I now give that attention to myself by showing up for my life.
—Robyn

11.

Self-Care Is the New Beautiful

Deep Gratitude and a Final Good-bye

By Robyn

Thirteen years ago, I stood on the other side of the world, where childhood memories rose to choke me with their finality, and good-byes that were not welcome came anyway.

My swollen hands rested on my mother's limp body. Every few seconds I would try to stroke the few parts of her not intruded upon by machinery. I was clumsy in my attempt to take in the essence of my mother before she, nineteen glorious years after the night she told our family she may be dying, finally left us. Her frail body shutting down as I stood beside her, full of life with baby kicking in time to her heartbeat that was kept going artificially. My hands fumbled around tubes and needles. I cried with the awareness that my mum, the woman whom I depended upon and who was my everything, was about to leave this world, one short month before my first child would be born.

My mum saw me for three years in recovery. She saw me marry the man I had fallen for in a way that she had never witnessed in the past. She saw the connection of soul mates in us, and then she saw me pregnant, something she had never envisioned because of the disorder. She saw her little girl's essence return, an essence that could create a bubble of laughter around her when she spoke. She saw me, the real me had returned home to her after my own battle with illness. I thank God so much for those three years. And of course, I wanted more time.

Becoming a mother myself, I know now that I soothed my mum's soul by being in recovery. I always got the sense that my mother would never leave me to fight a battle alone. I know as a parent that the love we have for our children is unconditional and deeper than any other love one can experience. I know the eating disorder and the emotional torture of questioning what part she may have had in it caused sleepless nights for her (and my father). Parents always question their part, even though they can't save their children from an eating disorder, for no one has that power. I saw my mum let go of that guilt and deep sadness for her child in the last three years of her life. I am so grateful that I have that to look back on now.

In the weeks prior to landing at her hospital bedside, I had a conversation with my mum during a warm Santa Monica night that will stay with me forever. I lay on my bed with only my head propped up feeling the breeze from our open window, the fear in my chest threatening to bubble up to the surface to paralyze us both. I breathed and prayed. Prayed and breathed. I'm sure she was doing the same.

Mum was struggling to breathe as the lupus attacked her lungs and told her body that her organs were not her own. Again, on the other side of the world, on the phone—this time, I was able to be there for her.

Mum was scared, and she told me so, an open dialogue I will treasure till my own death.

"I am scared, Robbie. But I just told God that I would go along for the ride." The amount of surrender in her facing of death was as equal to her fight when she was first diagnosed, and in kidney failure.

"Of course you are, Mum." I said. I remember being so conscious of needing to hear her, honor her truth, and love her to her death. I guess you could say this was a sign of my own newfound bravery in recovery. We both knew she was dying. It was an unspoken thing that my mother conveyed to me with her thoughts. We had always had that connection. Even on the other side of the world, my mum knew when something was wrong with me. She would call me and say, "What's wrong Robbie-Lou?" I now experienced that with her, and I comforted *her*.

"Oh, thank you, Robbie, you have made me feel so much better" was one of the last things she ever said to me. I am so grateful for recovery.

Nearly two weeks after arriving home from my mother's bedside, now thirty-six weeks along, I sat clad in old, plaid pajamas, the only item that provided my pregnant body comfort. Tim and I cuddled close on our sofa, with the TV acting as white noise. We weren't really watching anything; we were buying time until our life changed. Those last weeks of pregnancy had me nesting at home, making sure we had everything ready for our little soon-to-be Lilly, our own family. Then the phone rang. I knew it was my brother. It wasn't the "no caller ID" that came up on the blinking phone screen that gave it away, but the air of freeness that lingered around our tiny Santa Monica apartment. I believe it was the freeness of my mother's soul leaving her physical pain behind. We felt that. That. We felt *that*.

"She's gone, Bub," my brother croaked.

I couldn't speak, as the long-awaited death was now absolute. I took a breath and held my stomach as my mind froze with the shock. I mumbled something to my brother, and as I hung up the phone, holding my arms around my baby's bulge, I screamed with a primal, wounded rawness. And then I screamed again. I screamed in the hope of catching my mum's spirit as she passed beyond us, out of this lifetime. How can I continue to live? I thought. She's gone. She is *gone*. I let out a scream again, this time for my unborn children.

You see, the truth was, I *could* live, however unbearable that reality felt. The universe made it so with a baby of my own to live for. Life is mysterious and magical and painful all in one. I am blessed that my mum lived nineteen additional years from the day the doctor told her to tell her family of her imminent death. I am indebted that I had her to teach me what being a woman and a mommy meant. I take this with me now as I raise my own children. I am thankful that I hear her words, still, when I need advice; when I am still and so very quiet, I hear them. I am grateful that when she died, I became more of the woman I wanted to become through every step I took following my recovery. My mum was never again on the end of the phone, but her lessons were instilled deep within me. I learned to confide in myself, and I grew up because of it. I know she would be proud of me. I am grateful that she showed me what self-care looked like as she refused to give in to her illness. The measures she went to in order to care for herself now pave the way for me.

I am also grateful for my girls, who showed me the love my mum had for me. I understand that death is not something I should push myself toward for peace, but a sacredness beyond any mind's comprehension, one that is final. I am grateful that today I get to be present in a conversation after having eaten a meal; the meal has no power over me. Once eaten, it is over—period (just like it was meant to be). I am grateful that I understand now that I don't have any control over this world and the people and things in it; this responsibility and pressure to be in control is pointless and too heavy, anyway. I am grateful for the mystery in this life, and that even when I think I know; I often don't.

I take comfort in this world being so much bigger than I ever imagined, and that I am but a blip on the radar—and most days, that is enough for me. I take pride in letting go and seeing life on life's terms. I am grateful that I have the confidence to walk through anything and be okay, for I have walked through death, bankruptcy, an eating disorder, and depression. None have killed me; and yes, they have made me stronger. I have shut the door on the eating disorder behavior because it has no place or need in my life today. Today I walk through life, not fearless, not perfect, not knowing what is around the corner . . . but still okay.

And I could say that I carry the same sentiment about food today. Now that I know unequivocally that I can eat whatever I want when I am hungry and stop when I am full, I have also discovered how the actual foods make me feel—and the way I feel when consuming certain foods changes as my health changes, hormones change, or as I age. The Self-Care Approach to eating within *The Body Conversation* is the phase where I get to honor my body and its needs over the noise of our culture and latest fad diet craze. It's a phase that considers both my physical and mental nutritional needs and incorporates them into the Mindful Approach (Phase 2) without rigidity.

Over the years, I've discovered eating a pastry full of sugar for breakfast makes me tired by noon. I know that I need carbohydrates to sleep well. I know that oatmeal and apples are great to ward off heart disease and are very effective (along with exercise) to keep my cholesterol at bay. I know coffee on an empty stomach makes me anxious and too much dairy constipates me. Also, over the past few years, I've begun to increasingly dislike eating animal flesh. Being conscious about one's food will sometimes do that to us. I eat more fish and plant product these days, except when my body says it would like it.

One thing is still true for me though: Whenever I consider "cutting back" on foods I love, I always want to eat them more. I cannot diet, for with every diet, overeating awaits. Unfortunately, there are a lot of wages that are paid via the diet industry, so I need to have discernment for myself. Dieting for me is inviting self-sabotage, and usually means that I am out of touch with my body's mind and my emotional well-being. Emotional well-being is vital to my recovery.

The truth is, I may always have broken glasses (seeing my body in a way that is not real, but based only on my emotions.) When I get flooded with emotions or run-down and don't feel good about a situation, I tend to look in the mirror and see a large lady staring back at me. Over time, I've learned that the image in front of me in the mirror is more a reflection of my internal struggle than the real shape of my body. I don't buy into it. My body no longer owns my definition of self. Today, I am able to shift my perception of self without self-destruction, so that I can see my body more accurately.

I would not take back my process of food discovery and recovery, ever. I truly mean this. I have learned so much about myself through my food choices that now provide me with a strong foundation for my fully recovered life. But it wasn't enough not to be body obsessed anymore and to be able to eat whatever I wanted; I also craved optimum health. Optimum health is discovering what makes you feel your best and being capable of honoring it. I now cherish my life and my ever-growing zest for it, and want to be my best self in it.

There is a reason why this chapter is at the end of the book and not at the beginning: Maybe you feel like I once did. I could not have been truthful and curious about my body in a way that promotes optimum health when I was beginning recovery. My mind was not there yet. My body had lost contact with my mind years ago, and I needed to reconnect them first. I was able to via the Structured Approach, and strengthen the relationship via the Mindful Approach.

A while back I was involved in a discussion with two women of my extended family about one of their concepts of "good" and "bad" food. When one of the women said, "Robyn *loves* her food. With the amount she eats, she should be the size of a house." The other lady cringed, as I think she may have taken this comment to be careless, even hurtful, but I knew it was not really about trying to criticize me, nor was she commenting on *my* food intake as it *really* was. Like most of us, she has been taught our cultural "norm." You see, I think she may have been complimenting me. By saying that it was due to my genes that I was not fat, she was insinuating that I was a "lucky" woman who had dodged the bullet of having to watch every morsel that enters my mouth. The truth? She has been deceived by our society to believe that dieting is the answer to optimal health. Like most of us, she has been fed the lies instead of the truth of diets and their danger to bring us further away from our body's intelligence and make us feel emotionally overwhelmed in the process. My body structure was created from my gene pool, yes, but I also follow a general rule: If I am hungry and the food that is available to me is something my body wants, I eat it. Sometimes it is not what I want, but I have to eat something because my body is asking for it, so I make do and eat anyway. If I am not hungry, I don't eat. I no longer feel like "I have to eat it because tomorrow I can't." It's that simple, really. I am far from what my extended family member might call a "big eater," but yes, I do love my food. Dieting has become a part of our culture, but I don't have to buy into it or be a part of it. This is part of my self-care today.

Here's the thing about recovery and life: You'll have many people tell you what is right for you, even inside the eating disorder recovery community. Or you'll have the group that tells you that recovery must look a certain way—their way. That, in fact, your treatment should look a certain way, but only you and your treatment team decide that. You will have people saying that, if you choose to go gluten free for optimum health reasons, i.e., overcoming chronic constipation, irritable bowel, etc., then you are going into disordered eating behaviors.

It's taken me sixteen years to get to a point where my relationship with my body and God trumps the noise of all those who think they know the facts about me—but don't. As I say to my girls, "Darlings, the world is going to inundate you with telling you what you must look like, but if you build a relationship with your body where you listen, connect, and respond to it, and where you honor it, then what the outside world says to you about it is of no concern. Your body will guide you." After all, it's so intelligent that it can create life, so why the hell can it not tell you when it is hungry, what it needs, and when it's had enough? A truth barometer resides within us all.

Self-care is knowing the things that make me feel good about myself, that help me speak my truth and support my needs as an individual, and then acting on them to best honor myself. Self-care in all it represents is my new definition of beautiful. It's so much more fulfilling than the media's definition—so much more inspiring, liberating, and obtainable.

I understand that my body needs a certain amount of exercise, protein, sleep, hydration, fun, laughter, "me" time, quiet time, "Mommy, Lilly, and Chloe" time, "no computer" time, "Tim and Robyn" time, and good ol' "chit-chat with my best friend, Andi" time. Sometimes I still choose to have food that I have discovered I am sensitive to. But it's a conscious choice that is not laden with guilt or shame. I sense that, like everything, when I've had enough of the energy zaps I will let go of it organically. I try to encourage my little girls to eat this way too. There is no "good" or "bad" food in our house, just "energy" food and "fun" food. Our home has many "fun" foods within it that I do not think twice about today, for food has no power here anymore.

I know that self-care is in my pauses, in my willingness to give up the illusion of control. It is in being present, in being able to laugh at myself; it is in pursuing my dreams and loving to the best of my ability. I know this about me because *I now know me.*

How to Appreciate Something as a Path to Loving It

By Espra

What Does Self-Care Mean to You?

Eating Disorder Thought: "It means, 'Stop eating so much, you pig.'"

Truth: Self-care is a practice, and it is a wide path that shifts with the moment, circumstance, and life. It is the middle path, somewhere in the wide space between self-indulgence and self-deprivation.

Society, the media, and those around us give conflicting messages about self-care. Self-sacrifice, exhaustion, and productivity are viewed as qualities of a "good" person, while self-care, self-compassion, and self-kindness are seen as self-indulgent. Relying on others to decide what self-care means for you can leave you confused and vulnerable. Buying the eating disorder's self-deprivation mandates will ultimately destroy your body, heart, and mind.

When you get to this stage in your recovery, you can more readily tune in and respect the quiet voice inside you that knows depriving and punishing yourself does not create a life worth living. The challenge is to walk your personal path of self-care, notice when you stray to either side, then move back to it and just begin again. Remember, different standards for self-kindness and self-care do not apply to you just because you are "unworthy," "undeserving," or different than everyone else in any other way (that's eating disorder thinking).

From Perfection and Guilt to Curious and Proud

Eating Disorder Thought: "Once you're perfect, you can feel good about yourself. Self-compassion is an excuse for self-indulgence and laziness. Permission to do or be anything less than perfect opens the door to becoming the big, fat slob you deserve to be."

Truth: Believing these lies will pretty much guarantee that you remain loyal to the eating disorder. Breaking free requires doing the *opposite* of what the eating disorder thoughts are telling you to do or, in the words of my clients, "faking it till you make it."

Focusing on making yourself perfect leads you toward feeling guilty and miserable, not happy. As you move away from self-deprivation and perfectionism toward self-care, prepare for your eating disorder thoughts to deliver guilt and shame. The eating disorder thrives on your self-deprivation, telling you how bad you are and helping you always remember it. Eating disorders insist that depriving, judging, and punishing yourself are the only ways to keep you motivated to do what you are "supposed to do."

If you feel like you don't deserve to relax for ten minutes, relax anyway, because that quiet inner voice beneath the eating disorder's chatter knows it is helpful for you. Talk back, insisting that a life of meaning and quality is built upon developing pride in acting in congruence with your authentic self, not your rigid and inflexible self. If you are tired, go to bed earlier. If relaxing in bed is how you avoid your life, then get out of bed more often. Each moment brings a new chance for you to either batter yourself with guilt about your imperfections or orient yourself back toward the path of self-care. Beginning again means focusing your mind on being curious about both the pleasant and the scary things that lie beyond your bed, instead of punishing yourself for having been there in the first place. As you replace your self-deprivation rituals with intuitive and authentic actions, you begin living from authentic power and diminishing the power of the eating disorder. Everything, initially, will feel like self-indulgence. Work hard to mold your thinking from guilt and obsession with perfection at any cost, into curiosity and the kind of pride each of us finds in self-respect.

Your Body, Acceptance, and Appreciation

Eating Disorder Thought: "Are you joking? Now they're trying to convince you that you're hallucinating when you see your own body."

Truth: Individuals who suffer with eating disorders are at high risk of having "broken glasses," which cause them to see their body as twenty-five percent, thirty percent, or as much as double its actual size or more.

Questioning your perception of the size and shape of your body is frightening but important.

Robyn understood and worked to accept that a symptom of her eating disorder was that she literally saw the size and shape of her body as completely different than its actual size or shape. This is a symptom of an eating disorder that is called body dysmorphia. Part of healing is beginning to trust that you see your body as larger than it actually is. The resulting self-consciousness and obsessive preoccupation with your body are consuming to the point that even conversations and activities can become miserable and seemingly impossible. Feigning interest while being distracted by checking and hiding your body's flaws is exhausting, and many with eating disorders avoid people and activities as much as possible.

To compound the problem, another characteristic of eating disorders is placing a greater emphasis on the shape or size of your body than on other aspects of yourself as the means of determining your personal value and worth. You are in quite a fix. You are at risk of seeing your body as larger than it actually is, and what you see in the mirror defines you as worthless and disgusting. To say that the eating disorder has set you up to be miserable is an understatement.

Not yet satisfied, as usual, the eating disorder carries on to convince you that the rest of the world also notices, stares, and feels disgusted by you. This is another lie. Yes, some people do judge our bodies and other things they dislike about us because some people are just that way and our culture encourages this type of objectifying of others and ourselves as just a body. But the ways in which others judge you are rarely as horrific as your eating disorder would have you believe or as those assaults the eating disorder personally delivers to you. Talk back: How many people have you observed running out of the room and gagging immediately after you walk in? Others tend to be put off more by someone who's preoccupied with their own body than the size of that person's body. When you are preoccupied with comparing bodies, looking at your reflection, and adjusting your body and clothes, people lose interest in being around you because they feel unimportant and ignored. Logical conclusion: It is more likely that your behaviors, rather than your appearance, make others feel awkward and uncomfortable around you. Perhaps it's the eating disorder, not your body that is undesirable to others. Think about this and talk back!

Because you see your body with your own two eyes (though your vision is probably distorted), others cannot convince you that they view your body or you differently than you do. Recovery means educating yourself about your broken glasses, then constantly reminding yourself that body dysmorphia is a symptom of eating disorders, yours included. Work with your therapist and other resources to find concrete ways to challenge your view of your body rather than reducing yourself to an object. Questioning your perception of the size and shape of your body is frightening but important. Ironically, improving self-esteem, rather than losing weight, is the treatment for body dysmorphia. Broken glasses can be mended as you build gratitude, appreciation, and curiosity for how your body works and what it can do.

 Write a list of things you can do because you have a body. Review and appreciate these things once or more each day.

Examples: Hug someone, look at the ocean, feel the sun on my face, pet my dog, listen to music, walk in nature, play a sport, or fly a kite.

Discover for yourself how appreciating the body you have, not pushing to make it a certain way, is the key to happiness. A client of mine once said, "I love my body because it is strong and performs well for me. But I hate the way it looks." You may never love your body, and, honestly, few people do. The key to creating a life worth living is getting curious about your body and the miracle of it. When you teach yourself to appreciate the ways your body helps you live a meaningful life and use your body to do just that, you break free from seeing yourself as nothing but an object and having to rely on your appearance to measure your worth. You accept the body you have, appreciate what it can do for you, and love it for showing up for you. You are not an object whose worth is based solely on how you look. You are not a size or weight. Refuse to spend your time, energy, and passion trying to reduce yourself to any number. You are a human being. You are something. You matter.

Tier Three: The Self-Care Approach to Eating

Eating Disorder Thought: "That's easy. Self-care means eating healthy. Otherwise you'll look gross."

Truth: The research is clear. Health problems that have traditionally been blamed on "weighing too much" are more often related to imbalance in lifestyle than weight itself. Period.

> **The Self-Care Approach is both mindful and structured eating, not self-depriving or rigid eating.**

Our Self-Care Approach to eating considers structure and your preferences, but also moves beyond them to target your body's chemical and biological idiosyncrasies and ever-changing needs. You are ready for the Self-Care Approach when your emotions or worries related to food or your body's appearance no longer drive your choices. For the most part, fear is replaced by faith in your body and your ability to care for it in your human, imperfect, evolving, and curious way.

The Self-Care Approach is eating for optimum health. The Self-Care Approach is both mindful and structured eating, not self-depriving or rigid eating. You must be well practiced in both the Structured Approach and the Mindful Approach to eating before you attempt the Self-Care Approach.

Note: We suggest at least a year of practicing the Structured Approach and at least another year practicing the Mindful Approach before you consider incorporating the Self-Care Approach.

You can't skip the structured and mindful eating stages, as they decrease fears of food and teach making food choices to build self-trust, which is the essence of what you will ultimately need to quiet the eating disorder. The Self-Care Approach is the next step, as it helps you tune in to your unique body's responses to food over time. You may discover relationships between things like food types and amounts; times of the day, month, and year; and how they affect your body. This helps you shift (not restrict) what you eat and when you eat it to fit your needs at the time. The Self-Care Approach is not an invitation for orthorexia or disordered eating based on preoccupation with eating "healthy" food. This is unhealthy and imbalanced.

With the Self-Care Approach, you loosely use structure with times of day and a range of foods. You know you like some foods more than others; you accept that you can eat what you want without guilt and now you will begin to discover how different foods give your body advantages or disadvantages that others do not. You become curious about how foods affect your emotional, mental, and physical status and begin to make choices in eating the foods that make you feel good in the big picture. You can start to listen beyond your desires for certain foods, when your body becomes hungry. For example: If you need energy, attend to your body's messages about foods that give you energy, immediate and/or long-lasting. The antithesis of self-care is using certain foods, like caffeine or sugar, as "drugs" to give you a quick buzz of energy. *And* self-care for you might mean having caffeinated drinks and sweet or "carb-filled" foods when they sound good, or might give you a quick, fleeting energy surge, while being mindful that it is a choice rather than a thoughtless habit or pattern.

The Self-Care Approach is about recognizing what foods do for and to you. It's about using your nutrition to provide you with optimal physical, mental, and emotional functioning and wellness (according to your body's responses, not eating disorder reactions). Optimal physical functioning can be measured by things like energy that lasts longer than otherwise, increased strength, more even mood

The eating disorder is not a member of your healthcare team.

and emotional responses, clearer thinking, and your body feeling at ease. For example, when I crave ice cream, I try to honor my desire for sweet, cold, and creamy while staying mindful that my stomach will become bloated from milk and my joints will be more sore tomorrow. I also recognize that if I go for the ice cream in the middle of my work day, a time where I need more lasting energy, it will most likely not benefit my productivity. Using the Self-Care Approach I am able to consider my outcomes and make my choices accordingly, but not restrict my range of foods or feel deprived in the long run. Self-care eating is about being able to make these choices without the eating disorder nudging or interfering. Instead of ice cream, I may decide to go for yogurt that provides more lasting energy yet honors my body's desire for a sweet, cold, and creamy texture at the time, then, if I still want it, have ice cream later. Decisions need to be made between you and your body, and if necessary, your healthcare provider. The eating disorder is not a member of your healthcare team.

You find true freedom from the eating disorder as you move from its directives of "healthy" or "what you deserve" to your own body's wisdom of true nutritional self-care. Your blueprint for nutritional recovery must include the full repertoire of nutritional responses in life. Whether you are in a situation where you have many or only a few food options, you use what is available to refuel your body when needed. The eating disorder would have you either run your tank dry, waiting for the "perfect" fuel source, or indiscriminately fueling up, possibly overflowing your tank with little deliberate preparation. The Self-Care Approach is eating to keep your body, brain, and chemistry working optimally throughout the day. Using your Structured Approach skills, you "top off" every four or five hours even if not feeling hunger sensations to keep your body at an even level. Using your Mindful Approach, you are less afraid to top off with more food if you are hungry and less if you are not. You choose what your body wants from the range of food options available, and you use what is available when needed. After practicing the Structured Approach sufficiently, it becomes a natural, safe place. You own your Structured Approach. It is yours; it never fails and never goes away, as long as you are willing to go back to it when necessary. Robyn says that the foundation of her Structured Approach is now an ingrained part of her that she naturally falls back upon. When she is sick and her appetite decreases, Robyn knows that her Structured Approach is part of her way back and says, "It's quite brilliant, really, to have the solution within myself." Can you see how the Structured Approach *is* the Self-Care Approach? As long as you remember this, your body's mind will be capable of returning you to the Mindful Approach then the Self-Care Approach.

 Watch your physical responses to the foods you eat for one day. Keep track of what you notice is happening with your body, mind, and mood with respect to the foods you eat and when you eat them. Examples: Does your body respond with a quick rush? Improved mental clarity? Do you feel less sluggish? Irritable? Do you have more energy or endurance? Does your energy crash? Are you shaky, tired, washed out, weak?

After you gather this information about your body's responses to certain foods, you are positioned to experiment, and the next time you are hungry make a conscious choice that may result in

what you need at the time. You are not locked into always making choices this way. In fact, sometimes you won't. Sometimes I do eat ice cream for lunch, and I enjoy it. This is choice. This is power.

For example: When I'm taking a long hike and stop for a break, I know that I need to have a little bit of candy, salty food, and jerky. I might not like the taste of the salty food that I brought, but I know I need to eat it anyway. The salt protects my electrolytes, the sugar gives me immediate energy to resume hiking, and the protein brings a delayed, longer-lasting energy for my body to use after the energy from sugar is spent. However, if I am sitting at a desk all day doing research, I may not make the same food choices.

Warning: If the eating disorder is poking you and whispering, "Hey don't forget about 'good,' 'bad,' 'diet' or 'binge' foods," don't panic. It's okay; you've come a long way. Just notice that you feel unsafe or anxious then bring your mind back to a recovery mindset, your wise mind, and go back to the Mindful Approach, or if necessary, the Structured Approach to eating until you have regained your physical and mental stability with food.

Wake Up and Show Up

Eating Disorder Thought: "Yes, why don't you wake up their way and see what shows up . . . on your thighs. No one will show up."

Truth: Can you now begin to move beyond the eating disorder's focus only on your body as a way to show up in life? There is no guarantee that your body will or won't change from improved self-care, but I am convinced that your life will change for the better.

As you learn to listen to your body, your heart and your mind take their places in the balance of your life. As you express your true desires and live your life based on what is in the best interest of your mind and body, the voice of the eating disorder begins to have less power over you. You will find its chatter less believable, your ability to challenge it increases, and the percentage of your day that it talks and your behaviors obey it decreases.

As your head clears and your behavior is not consumed by the eating disorder thoughts, you become able to look around you and see outside of yourself. You are opening your eyes and taking in information from your environment, versus your heart or head exclusively. You wake up to your world. You wake up to life.

Now your recovery, instead of the eating disorder, is starting to take on a life of its own. Now you can sincerely listen, hear without distraction, see, and respond to your life. Your relationships deepen and become more meaningful . . . not because you have created a perfect body, but because you are showing up. You are attentive instead of constantly comparing yourself to others. You are finding things to discuss other than food, calories, bodies, and exercise. People are responding to you because you are more interesting to be around. When you live in a place of self-care, you do not eat perfectly; you eat imperfectly while showing up (for yourself and others) and expressing yourself in a perfectly imperfect way. You are perfectly human, and you immerse yourself in the enduring things that matter to you most in the context of your long-term goals and values.

Sometimes when talking with clients who embrace Christianity, I imagine them standing at the "pearly gates"; St. Peter is there asking them to step on a scale to determine whether or not they will be allowed into heaven. When put this way, does it start to sound a little bit ludicrous to think your self, essence, worthiness, and entire life are reduced to a number or size? I cannot imagine this is anything related to the point or meaning or purpose of a human's life on this earth. I'm convinced it is to create, find, and be your own kind of beautiful and to see it in others.

Playing it safe is like poking yourself in the eye.
Ultimately you lose sight of all the magic around you.

Today, I will allow myself to take
part in the world around me.
Life is worth my attention. I am worth the world!
—Robyn

12.

Make Recovery Worth It

Dreams and Bottom Drums

By Robyn

Although recovery has long been entrenched in my bones and my thought process naturally steers toward it, I am sometimes still fascinated by the odd sensation of looking back at my behavior during the eating disorder and being unable to grasp what kept me in a life near death and trapped for so many years.

Every now and then, I'll be at my desk working or taking a run around our local parks, and I'll flash back to the grief that once burdened me daily. For a moment, I will be pulled right back into the memory: a bout of purging or panic attacks induced by malnourishment or exhaustion, or waking up after a binge or to a stranger after a night out drinking. I get lost in it.

Sometimes, too, I recall the pain I inflicted on those who loved me the most while in my disorder, and although the guilt and shame can sometimes still catch me unaware, I no longer allow myself to remain stuck in pain. Recovery doesn't ask us to beat ourselves up endlessly. Instead, it offers us a chance to have as many do-overs as we need. Today, I get to reach out to those I love, without guilt or shame, and show up in the way I wanted to so desperately in the disorder—pretending to be no one other than me.

The beginning of the recovery journey is slow and often messy. If you had told me sixteen years ago that I could feel the way I do today, I would have called you a liar. I would have told you that you don't know me or my body; therefore, you couldn't possibly tell me that I could do it. If you knew me better, you would understand. I'd remind you that I am part European, prone to curvy hips, lady mustaches, and a mix of a deep, dark depression that, if exposed, might kill me. "So let me be," I would have warned you, with a look that would distance you in a heartbeat. *Let me be.* I am destined to walk this life chained to my fateful eating disorder, worthless, alone, and hopeless.

But now I am telling you that you too can feel recovery! I don't care what you say is different about you. Eating disorders do not discriminate. We are the same, and you too can be free from it and the underlying issues that may hide beneath it, if you want to be.

One of the questions I have asked myself is, "What does recovery mean to me?" Recovery, for me, means showing up for myself and others. Recovery means being able to be present. It means accepting imperfections and life on life's terms. It means feeling my feelings, and with that, experiencing real pain, real discomfort, real happiness, laughter, hope, and . . . me. Recovery means experiencing the sensation of running, but standing still anyway. It means laughing at myself sometimes. It means being open to the magic of our glorious and sometimes scary world. I reflect on this to remind myself of what I can do now that I could not do when my life was dictated by body image and eating disorder anguish. When I get quiet and find one thing that recovery means to me, other gifts, other things that I can do in recovery flood in on me until a sense of gratitude permeates my being.

Recovery does not mean that life will be perfect from now on. Being perfect or striving for it is not what my recovery is about. The pursuit of perfection brings with it similar sensations to that of an eating disorder. I run from it like a burning building. Albeit, sometimes I still have to feel the burn of the flame before I decide to run, but I do end up running. I say no to eating disorder and no to perfection.

Recovery does not mean that I no longer have to work on myself. I don't hide from the fact that there are underlying issues such as trauma, depression, anxiety, and other difficulties that I need to trudge through as part of my recovery, as part of life. I have come to believe that, for me, life is really about returning home to myself. I have learned to do this by rediscovering the way to connect to myself, to others, and to an energy far beyond me.

There is no destination in recovery, no point we hit in our journey where we will never struggle again. However, "Pain is inevitable, but suffering is optional." One of the beautiful gifts of recovery is not that you will never struggle, but rather . . . *We get to choose whether we suffer or not.* We choose whether we go deeper into the hurt and through it or whether we sit and suffer, toward self-destruction or away from it. Recovery is a choice, and so is suffering. I still can suffer, of course, and sit in it for far too long. It's just that I don't tend to sit in it as long anymore, and making a fatal U-turn is no longer an option.

A couple of years ago, entrenched in the canals of recovery, I looked like I had it all—a dream career, traveling the United States advocating and educating about eating disorder recovery, a book release, a marriage I was still in (I find commitment a little difficult), and two thriving daughters. I had reached this point by, yes, being in recovery (without it, I am clear that I could not obtain or keep any of it), but it also was because I busied myself until I couldn't busy myself any longer.

One September night as I lay awake next to my husband, my scalp was burning and my thoughts were zapping like a swarm of mosquitos. I couldn't catch them. Not one. I sat upright, grinding my teeth. I had been in a panic for days with no sign that it would end. My thoughts frightened me. *Would I go crazy and hurt myself? Would I hurt others?* With each thought, the panic spiked even further. I never knew panic could last that long, or that my body could tolerate it. It felt like the lions were lurking, and I was about to be eaten.

Months ago, I did not heed the warning. Correction: I did not heed the copious warnings. I could no longer tell the difference between a stick and a snake. I was in a pit of snakes as far as my panic was concerned. So, by the time I got to that September night, I lay awake suffering profoundly.

It's not that we will never find ourselves suffering, but we will come to understand that there is an alternative. We can ask for help.

I woke up my husband and said, "Baby, I'm struggling so bad."

"What do you mean?" he asked, groggy with sleep.

"I'm having panic attacks, and they're not ending. I can't handle it anymore," I sobbed.

"What do you mean, *anymore?*" He opened one of his eyes.

"I mean, I've been struggling for months," I said impatiently. However, now Tim was impatient too, and angry—or at least irritated.

People may get upset with us when we suffer in silence because they may become scared that we are hurting ourselves and they had no idea, and this brings up their own stuff. It can also make them wonder how can they help us if they don't know. However, those are their feelings. We don't need to save them when we are trying to save ourselves. We can take a deep breath and tell them we need help anyway.

"I just need you to hold me, and I will ask for help tomorrow," I said. I was already finding relief because I had shared my suffering with someone else, and crying helped dissipate the scary thoughts and panic trapped in my body. The next day, I challenged my own stigma about myself and asked for help. I was able to do this because I knew I had a choice.

The personal challenges that led me to hide from myself and my life are now the things I show up and face, albeit sometimes slowly. But the real payoffs for me, and I am as shocked as you may be, are the little things that make the showing up in recovery all worth it. Like when I hear the outside noise of birds getting on with their morning as they sit on the stripped branches of winter singing to all who will listen. Or when out of the blue, I feel uncomfortable and I can check in with myself, without the noise and violence of the eating disorder voice, and within moments, discover what is really going on. This makes recovery worth it for me.

When I can feel bored, impatient, frustrated, and less-than after looking at acquaintances' or strangers' (yep, I said it) social media pages without having to look in the fridge or the mirror. Instead, I call a friend, take a walk, ask for help, or sit with my feelings knowing that it will pass, if I allow it to. And when my little girls comment on the shape of my bottom and pat it like a drum, I can shake it off without feeling that I have failed. This peace and ease with who I am makes recovery, and indeed life, worth it.

It is not that life is magical *all* of the time. It would be cruel of me to say that my life is always grand and that all I have in my life is perfect. It's simply not true. In fact, sometimes I still feel larger than I am, and sometimes life feels messy, hard, and even a little (okay, a lot) unmanageable. I know these moments well. I also know the moments well of when these emotions pass because I understand now that when I feel vulnerable, my body feels larger, and nowadays, older, than it actually is. The difference today is on most days, I don't take those feelings to heart. I take action—action that centers me. I go back to basics, and I nurture myself in a way that makes me feel good about myself, not a way that punishes me for feeling imperfect.

In recovery I can be a part of a solution and a freedom and a peace that are just waiting for me to walk into and own. Life is fleeting. As I remind myself how I want to live it today, I know that I am all of the power I gave the eating disorder, and that's a hell of a lot of power! You have it too!

I also unequivocally know that I am enough. Doing my best is enough. I know that I don't and never will have all the answers in life, nor do I know what will come of my efforts. But putting my efforts into my dreams provides me with self-worth and self-esteem because I am finally doing everything I always wanted. I define my own worth, dreams, truth, power, and beauty.

You see, this is *my* life. I can make it a playground or a prison. It is my choice. It is my day.

Just as it is yours!

Create Your Own Drums

By Espra

Know What Recovery Means

Eating Disorder Thought: "You can eat, and you can stop getting rid of calories. You can also have a miserable life, because that's how recovery will be."

Truth: A life of value, quality, and meaning grows from saying no to the eating disorder.

Most of my clients have been afraid that recovery would mean a lifetime of abstaining from eating disorder behaviors while being battered by the barrage of eating disorder thoughts and feelings of misery. Although it seems impossible to live without eating disorder behaviors and with less misery, both are possible. In fact, the less you practice eating disorder behaviors, the more the chatter backs off. But do not expect the eating disorder's chatter and lies to die out right away. It takes time for the chatter to diminish, so please don't give up when you become frustrated that it does not back off as quickly as it "should." The eating disorder's assaults will actually increase initially, known in psychology as an "extinction burst," before it begins to back down. Then, even as it retreats, it will return to batter you in waves. But if you pay careful attention, you will probably be able to observe that its assaults, gradually and with time, decrease in intensity, frequency, and/or duration. Robyn and I cannot even promise you that they will ever be extinguished, but we know they will get better. I wish I created this phenomenon because then I could change it. The best I can do is explain how the eating disorder will behave as you challenge it. So be sure to acknowledge that you are changing.

Since no one in their right mind would pursue recovery without real reasons to do so, keep the reasons you are seeking recovery alive in your mind by frequently referring back to the tools you have used throughout this book. You will be extremely uncomfortable in the earlier parts of recovery, as new ways of interacting with the eating disorder and your world throw you out of the status quo and into a sort of chaos. For a while, the new ways will not feel comfortable, so you may go back to habitual patterns. But soon the old, familiar patterns will become less comfortable, leaving you feeling like neither your new behaviors nor your old ones fit. Stay with the discomfort, and the new ways will become new patterns and habits; they will become the new status quo.

Research shows that a complete recovery from eating disorders is possible. Many of my clients have proven to themselves and to me that recovery is possible. Like Robyn, you will become less dependent on the eating disorder's illusions that being "skinny," "perfect," or sick is the only way to get your needs met. You will become more capable as you cultivate the skills to meet your needs in ways that are more skillful and effective and less destructive to yourself and those around you. No matter what your eating disorder may tell you, a full and complete recovery is attainable, not only for others, but also for you.

No matter what your eating disorder may tell you, a full and complete recovery is attainable, not only for others, but also for you.

Shortly after Robyn heard that she should be as big as a house due to what she eats, Robyn called me. When Robyn told me what happened, my words hit no speed bumps before rushing out to ask what she thought and felt about those words. I wondered if she had flashes of guilt or shame, and if those brought up eating disorder thoughts or urges to restrict or purge. Robyn told me that she did notice a thought: "With the amount that I eat, I should be exactly the size that I am, thank you very much." She walked away from that situation without contempt for herself or her body, but with sadness for what society so convincingly teaches us—that self-deprivation and "self-control" is the only way to have a body that is "good enough" to make the person "good enough." I was already clear, but if there was any doubt remaining, I was certain at that moment that Robyn had fully recovered from her eating disorder.

Dislike for our bodies and thoughts of inadequacy still show up among the other irritating thoughts we all occasionally have. The difference is that now they won't grab your attention, emotions, or behavior in the same way . . . and they certainly won't run your life. Society will not stop trying to impose its rules on you as if you were an object and trying to force your body into an unrealistic mold to be good enough. As you identify those things of higher meaning and value in your life, you are no longer at the mercy of the eating disorder's illusions. You will notice the thoughts of inadequacy and keep right on doing whatever you are doing in that moment. You will keep living your life, striving to immerse yourself in the preciousness of the very moment you are in—before the moment is lost forever.

Know What "Worth It" Means

Eating Disorder Thought: "The only way you can be happy without me is to be happy being a body size you never wanted to become."

Truth: The only way to be happy without the eating disorder is to be willing to be without the eating disorder.

By now you know that the eating disorder has insane expectations about perfect bodies and controlling eating. You know the eating disorder moves the finish line as soon as you cross it, insisting that its prior goal is no longer good enough, and you have to do even more and be better. It can move that bar until death do you part.

Both joy and suffering are parts of all of our lives. Happiness is more a state of mind than an emotion. What makes recovery worthwhile is your ability to live a life that aligns with your long-term goals and values. It is a sort of peace and relaxing into your life. It is being our authentic selves with others, regardless of the outcome. Recovery is worth it when you begin to have faith in your ability to navigate rather than numb emotions. Recovery is worth it when you fully experience your life.

Play. Enjoy. It's Your Life!

Eating Disorder Thought: "Playing is a waste of time. You need to do things that are meaningful and worthwhile."

Truth: That which is meaningful and worthwhile can only be defined by you and can only be defined based on your core values and passions.

Planning pleasant things to do, big and small, doing them, and fully immersing yourself in them is part of the therapeutic treatment for shame and depression. Throw yourself in. Act interested and happy and, in the best-case scenario, you and those around you just might enjoy the experience. Worst-case scenario: it will go by faster if you are immersed in it.

Current research is exploding with information showing that "isolation and loneliness is the new smoking." In general, being isolated or lonely deteriorates physical and mental health and shortens the length of lives as much as smoking fifteen cigarettes per day. We are more disconnected from one another than ever with electronics and social media, and at a time when the eating disorder is working to convince you that the only safety lies in not being around others at all unless you are "thin enough" (by its standards), at a time when the eating disorder has you convinced that you are unworthy of love and connection . . . loneliness and isolation are reaching all time highs. Americans are reporting more loneliness now than ever before. Yet we need connection with others for support, checking our stories, and oxytocin that is necessary for survival.

Learning to be with others in the absence of the eating disorder's distorted thinking, talk, and behavior is yet another challenge and gift of recovery. As you show up physically, intellectually, and emotionally with other people, you identify those with whom you feel a sense of connection, trust, respect, and safety. The illusion that safety lies only in being loyal to the eating disorder grows fuzzy as you see glimpses of safety without it. The connection now begins between you and these caring others, as opposed to the isolation you experienced while at the mercy of the disorder. You are able to receive the gifts others bring to you, sort through what you do and do not want to accept, then truly give the gifts of your soul that endure beyond calories, food, and clothing size.

 Following the research of Rick Hanson, PhD, I have learned that creating a pleasant, safe, or connected experience is important. Being mindful as it occurs and knowing that it was good is also important. Brain research is showing that we need to take one more step. We need to install it in order to hardwire it into our brain, as positive events do not naturally stick. The way to do this is to call up the experience, gather any physical sensations we feel along with it, and take two breaths while holding that information. I have heard Dr. Hanson say, "This is how we can use our mind to change our brain." Try it. Look for any moments of connection, even brief, and try to "Install the Good" (the phrase coined by Dr. Hanson) at least twice a day. For a sample of this practice, watch Mr. Rogers' Emmy Acceptance Speech on YouTube. Mr. Rogers intuitively knew what brain science was going to teach us decades later.

Following Your Dreams
Eating Disorder Thought: "But, but . . . "
Truth: That's right.

Recovery is worth it when you have an idea of your passions, values, dreams, and goals, and you attend to them regularly, like tending a garden. As you sow your thoughts and actions, balanced emotions and healthy habits will blossom into maturity. Using the "Installing the Good" practice will plant positive experiences that will grow as well. Your garden will continue to need regular work and attention, but perfection is not necessary. Then, one day, it will seem like out of nowhere, you see evidence that you are reaping the ultimate harvest—a life of value and meaning that feels worth living. And it all becomes possible as *you* see and *you* acknowledge the eating disorder as the serious and real threat that it is to your life. It is like a devastating infestation of weeds that must be attended to. As you vigilantly challenge the eating disorder, you remove pieces of it from your life by the roots, like pulling one noxious weed at a time. Its ability to regenerate diminishes, and then halts. You must always pay attention for evidence that the eating disorder is returning so you can quickly challenge the devastating threats it will pose if it is allowed to propagate. It is important to cultivate and replant periodically, as conditions change. But one thing does not change: You are sowing the seeds that, when put all together, will bear more and more of what you ultimately desire over time.

> "Sew a thought and reap an act.
> Sew an act and reap a habit.
> Sew a habit and reap a lifetime.
> Sew a lifetime and reap a destiny."
> —*Anonymous*

Stay awake and attentive. We don't know exactly what your personal recovery will look like. We do know that recovery is a process of losing your way, noticing when you do, and, without self-punishment or denigration, getting right back on the path that takes you toward your authentic source of power. It is impossible for you to perfectly follow the path of living your dreams, values, and goals because you are human. Just don't quit. Find ways to keep your eyes on the path that takes you where you want to go. You deserve a life that feels worth living. You are strong enough to get there, and it is fully possible for you.

Structure your nutrition in order to stabilize your body. Respect the reality: Your body needs nutritional fuel and care. Then create peace with your body and food by cultivating peace with yourself. Practice mindful eating and self-care in eating and in your life. Use your authentic power to challenge the eating disorder's illusions of power, over and over again. Don't try to recover alone and don't give up. Perfection is an illusion. Trust is all you have to go on for now. The only way to see and touch the gifts that await you is to take a deep breath and jump in. Living a life of purpose, value, and meaning rather than living as a servant to a ruthless master we call the eating disorder is available to you.

Breaking through the mountain—
rubble hitting, hurting, shocking
my head, my body, my spirit.
I want to give up.
Yet I want to live.

I can turn back,
but when I look forward
I can see something.
I am not sure what it is.
But I know there is something.

With a deep breath
I move one foot

in front of the other.

Not with resistance.

It is with trust

and the tools I have found

along the way.

Something—

happiness, I think...

is waiting for me on the other side.

To all of you seeking recovery, you
are well on your way now.
                                        —Robyn

Epilogue

The Color Gray and One Converted School Bus

By Robyn

A lot can happen in seven years. That's the amount of time between Espra and I writing the first edition of this book and this one. Since then life has shown me that recovery is not only in the actions I take toward it, but in letting go of the illusion of control.

Letting go has always been frightening for me. Long into recovery, there have been times where my fearful thoughts held me hostage. The rapid motor of anxiety within will always assume leadership in my life and decisions if I allow it. Hand on heart, I will no longer allow it.

Last year, sixteen years into my recovery, I was waking up most mornings waiting for the anxiety engine within to blow its top, where it would finally, *finally*, render me "crazy." *How can this be? Why is it okay for me to still be dictated by fear long into my "recovery"? How can I play an active part in my life, rather than giving in to anxiety?*

It was anxiety that commenced long before eating disorder behavior, maybe even before Mum got sick, and it continued way after eating disorder behaviors were removed. I didn't want to find myself toward the end of my life feeling like I led my entire human existence attempting to outrun anxiety and panic attacks, and the fear surrounding them. I think my dad may have lived some, if not much, of his life like that too.

My dad grew up in a time where stigma kept secrets alive, not people. Men were taught to never speak about feelings or ask for help. Being a man meant sucking it up. We can speak about it now—more so than we ever have in history. There is more help available for you and I than there ever was for my father's generation. I feel both grateful and a responsibility to end this cycle for myself, my dad, and my girls.

Anxiety is crippling; it will keep us stuck in our homes, saying no to things that may have brought us deep joy, ending dreams too soon, making life decisions from a place of fear as opposed to hope, and it can also inhibit our connections with others. I wanted my recovery to be more than simply building a new relationship with food, body, and substances. I wanted it to represent fearlessness, and joy—a lot of it. That's the ultimate recovery I longed for!

In the winter of 2018, my family and I had just returned home from a vacation in Australia. It was summer there, full of family and old friends gathering and shoulder-tap reminders of my childhood dreams—the days of acting, of exploring, of hope. It's not that I don't have hope today. I do. Nor is it that I don't enjoy what I do for a living. I do, very much so. It's just that sometimes, I wonder what my life would have looked like if I hadn't given up acting, on a world so large that I use to dream about, determined to create, when I was a child—before life had its way with me and I forgot who I really was. Did fear influence my decision to quit acting when I entered recovery? Honestly, I don't know, but I'm leaning toward it. I suspect it was a combination of low self-worth, a sense of scarcity, and yes, fear too. For the record, recovery should not have you giving up on your dreams. It should inspire you to move toward them.

Our time in Australia was a stark contrast to six months before when I traveled there alone to help my brother and sister-in-law place Dad into assisted living. He had just turned seventy-three years old. It seemed so young to be needing assistance. I couldn't help but reflect on my life, on choices I've made and how I am living it.

The decision to place Dad in assisted living was partly because, a couple of years back, he had a stroke and lost his peripheral vision; then recently, he had spent eight weeks in the hospital due his skin breaking down. He looked like a burn victim and had to be bandaged to prevent scratching. Even the specialists claimed they were not sure what he had, even after many tests. But no matter what it was, Dad's kidneys had been functioning at a very low level, his liver was damaged, and he'd been diagnosed with diabetes. Although he'd tried to look after himself after his stroke, he needed support to do it.

Dad abided by an old narrative that told him that accepting help meant accepting he was "crazy," "less than," "weak." He is none of these; he never was. The narrative in which he lived told him, if he shared his secrets, he would be exposed to others' judgment and they would use those vulnerabilities against him. To be fair, stigma surrounding mental illness and addiction is still alive and thriving. It is in our systems, our workplaces, our communities, our doctors' offices, and our families.

The more we talk about our stories the more we can end stigma. Sharing our stories and asking for help should not be considered "brave." The use of such word suggest that mental illness is somewhat immoral and implies that those of us who have it are broken and need to be repaired in order to fit in with society. Those same connotations do not arise when sharing about needing help or sharing about one's physical ailments. Sharing our stories and asking for help surrounding mental health should be an everyday conversation.

Dad's strength was, and still is, evident. He kept himself alive, enduring debilitating anxiety and trauma, the best way he knew how. Anxiety, depression, and trauma left untreated will eat at us both mentally and physically, and maybe even lead us to living a life we did not wish for.

Leaving Dad and knowing he was unhappy with where he was hit me hard. Then upon returning to the United States the second time, with my family, I couldn't escape the nagging question, "What do you want your life to look like at seventy-three?" There was no mistaking that the difference between Dad and me was that I got the help I needed for my mental health. I was not so unlike him. Not just our genes; I also internalized a great deal of stigma toward myself. It was this stigma that prevented me from wanting to seek help for my paralyzing panic attacks until they hit a critical level, long into the eating disorder recovery and my career as a mental health advocate.

Not long after returning from our family vacation, I pushed myself into work. I knew I was emotionally and physically exhausted from the past year. I'd been traveling all over the country to train professionals on how to recognize eating disorder behaviors in those diagnosed with substance use disorder and on *The Body Conversation* model. I was also hosting social media sites with 250,000 followers who were struggling with eating disorders for the company I work for, and overseeing marketing strategies. Not to mention, most importantly, I was a mom and a wife. Even though I was tired (because, let's face it, when vacationing with family, many of us need a vacation from the vacation), I was too afraid to slow down. Slowing down felt unsafe.

One afternoon, I stood in the kitchen in our home in Denver, Colorado. If you had told me as a child that I would be living in Colorado for ten years of my life, I would have laughed. But, there in my kitchen, with the snow turning to ice outside my window in the Colorado sunshine, it was my reality—along with a fresh new cycle of panic attacks.

My body shook with a zapping sensation. Spikes of electricity shooting up my spine and throughout my scalp made me feel like I was on fire. My mind shifted from one scary thought to another. I stood with my bare feet on the wooden floor feeling hopeless.

You need to call Dr. Kirk, Robyn. It's time to ask for help. My wise-self (the part of me I know I could trust) said to me internally.

I shouldn't have to ask for help. I answered back with the part of me in fear—and yes, personal stigma.

Asking for help is a sign of strength, not weakness, Robyn. Remember? My wise-self reminded me.

I should be over having panic attacks by now. My fearful-self said.

It's okay that you're not. Wise-self responded.

What will people think of me if they find out that I need help? Me. A mental health advocate. I should have it figured out by now. Fearful-self fretted.

Then it struck me, giving fresh life to the panic: *Robyn, if you, a mental health advocate struggle with stigma still, how must the people you want to help feel about asking for help?* Zing. Zing. Zing. My fingers pulsated. Not only was fear dictating my life, it was exhausting me into panic. Now, I was being forced to take time out, and take stock of the way I was choosing to live that perpetuated my illness.

◆ ◆ ◆

Ever since I was a child, my dad wanted us to travel. From being a truck driver to riding on trains, my Dad had always dreamt of traveling across Australia for leisure. He dreamed of taking time out for his artwork, painting the landscapes he encountered along the way, such as the great snowy mountains and the waves of the Gold Coast. He didn't get to do the retirement trip he wanted, though. He got as far as buying the caravan (trailer), and then he put it off. There never seemed to be enough time or money. Then, he had the stroke and lost part of his vision, so he was unable to drive, or even paint like he used to. Not driving has been a heartache for Dad. Not painting another. Trucks and art were his life, his way of experiencing freedom. I no longer wish to put my life off. I no longer want to live in fear, and I sure as hell no longer want to tell others to ask for help while I don't, and instead choose to live in fear because I am scared that I will be perceived as less than or weak. I no longer want to play a role in perpetuating stigma. I no longer want to play a role in feeling trapped. Recovery demands we grab on to life or be dragged.

Tim and I have been mental health advocates for many years now. Tim has always been a lot bolder with his words than I am. You will often find him on social media discussing mental health policies and challenging the status quo of recovery. I've always been too scared that I would ruffle feathers if I didn't make sure what I said was on par with the messaging of those whom I considered authorities on the matter. I've come to understand that change doesn't happen like that though. I'm coming out of my shell. There is a lot to change when it comes to access to care and ending stigma throughout the recovery communities. Tim's passion and bravery inspire me daily.

Tim believes that, as John Travis says, "Connection is the currency of wellness." So, when we returned back home to Denver, we thought about how we could take our advocacy efforts to the next level as a family. We began to ask ourselves how could we connect with people who needed help and how could we be a part of change, starting with us. That's when we decided to get outside of our comfort zone to help change the perceptions of those struggling with mental illness and addiction, while also dealing with my own—my anxiety.

For a year, Tim and I planned a road trip that would have us selling our home, homeschooling our girls, converting a Thomas school bus into a tiny home, and traveling the United States to help end the stigma, and in turn, change the current narrative of mental illness and addiction. We wanted to explore ways that we could make mental health a part of an everyday conversation. With this in mind, the mental health initiative of Wide Wonder was born.

Wide Wonder consisted of twenty "throwing-stigma-under-the-bus" events around the United States, countless one-on-one meetings with community members and non-profit mental health organizations, and a lot of soul searching.

Full transparency, my advocacy trip around the USA is also self-serving—not just in the way of confronting my anxiety head on, but it's also a chance for me to return to my creative roots in Los Angeles. Our friends, family, and the mecca of the acting world are all there, and I want to be a part of it in some way. I don't know in what way yet, or if, when the reality hits the ideal, I'll even want it. But having the chance to find out is the greatest gift I could give myself. This is a gift of recovery. I want to "see" how it makes me feel. As my therapist said, "Seeing opposed to making is the key." Making something happen promotes the need to hustle. Seeing promotes curiosity.

Our family has been on the road for nine months now, and I've had my share of anxiety. On the bus, I've had plenty of chances to deal with my anxiety differently. From major bus breakdowns, to marriage squabbles and teen challenges, to homeschooling and my workload—I soon found that it wasn't just my anxiety that was the problem, but the old narrative within me that perpetuated it. Soon my anxiety turned to panic attacks. Then the panic attacks turned to intrusive thoughts.

Our family has traveled from Denver to Texas; from New Mexico to Arizona; then California, Washington, and Montana. To Iowa and Illinois; Maine and Boston; and then to New York. Everywhere I went the anxiety followed. In Maine, I finally told Tim (who I had now been married to for fifteen years) that I struggled with intrusive thoughts.

"Wow," he said. "Why would you want to live that way? Why have you not gotten any help?"

He was right, of course. So, in New York City, as the lights flickered and people gathered (millions of them) on the streets that are so close together one could begin to feel claustrophobic, I asked for help. Recovery is like that. We must always be open to asking for help when we need it. Whether we have already gone to treatment and therapy or been in recovery for over sixteen years, there may be flare-ups that require us to ask for help.

On the bus, I've also had my share of a profound willingness to get out of the way to let life happen—watch it unfold instead of forcing it to a particular way. Forcing is exhausting. Most days, our plans change. The bus breaks down or events come up. The bus gets messy and sometimes feels unmanageable. The girls invite a friend to stay with us because they are lonely, and if there was any room for privacy before them coming on the bus, there surely isn't now. Repairs override our budget, business partnerships don't measure up, or family gets ill. You get the point. Letting go has been a masterful tool in my ongoing recovery process and is awesome for squashing anxiety.

I even got to combat two of my biggest fears while on the bus: flying and leaving my girls. When arriving in Washington DC, my brother called and let me know Dad was back in hospital. With much thought and a session with my Exposure Response Prevention (ERP) Specialist, I decided to return to Australia for a month to be with Dad. Life can get super big, and no amount of control will take away the hard stuff. But if we allow anxiety and fear to dictate our lives, it will most certainly rob us of the good stuff.

I suspect, long after our family has gotten off the bus, I'll still find myself in recovery because recovery is life. Recovery is a process that allows me to show up for my life and the choices I make within it. It doesn't mean that I will never face obstacles, or fears, or pain I cannot control. It means I get to be present for all of it fully, sometimes clumsily—and discover a richness that I would have never been able to if I allowed myself to stay stuck. In recovery, I have that choice. And yes, dear recovery warriors, so do you!

I wish you so much love and support. We've got this! We deserve this!

You can follow me @RobynCruze and our family's mental health advocacy efforts to end stigma and make mental illness and addiction recovery a part of an everyday conversation at:

www.widewonder.life

Facebook and Instagram @widewonder.life

Twitter: widewonder_life

From Black and White to Color

By Espra

In the seven years since Robyn and I partnered to complete the first edition of this book, I feel as if I have lived a lifetime. I had just moved to one of my favorite vacation spots thinking that if I love it so much, why not be there all of the time instead of just when I can break away? I love the red rocks and red sand with green and snowcapped mountains as a backdrop.

A colleague and mentor of mine dragged . . . I mean, encouraged me to get certified to teach the Daring Way™ shame resilience curriculum created by researcher, Brené Brown, PhD, LMSW. It is designed to teach people how to work through the pain of shame to Show Up, Be Seen and Live Brave™. She called one day and said, "This feels vulnerable to me, but I'm going to say it anyway. I'm in this training, and I keep thinking how much I would love for you to get certified and teach it with me." I said "certainly." Sure I was interested, but I was busy finishing a book, and I think I mostly said yes because that's likely to be my fatal flaw. She came back a couple of years later, right after I moved to Southern Utah, and offered to help me get to a training. I arrived at that training in my own shame shit storm (as they say in the Daring Way™ culture) wearing a shirt that said "Santa, is it too late to be good?"

I was so disconnected from my values that I didn't know how I was going to get back. And I had made promises to loved ones I had hurt to find some way to bring a better self forward. There I started on the deliberate path of being brave and authentic, and it absolutely changed my life. This work is so empowering and results in unbelievable connection with others! I now teach with that colleague three-day intensive workshops for shame resilience, the Daring Way™, and how to get back up when we fall face down in life, Rising Strong™, in the Salt Lake City area. It is fun.

It feels like my world has gone from black and white to color. I have more laughter, connection, love, and emotional closeness; less fear; children and grandbabies; and so much more. Although my dad was finally freed from the chains that bound him to this life on earth and I am so sad to be without him, I am so grateful that his voice, words, and love live with me every day, as does my mom's. I am truly blessed with love.

I cofounded and now run a program called Life Launch Centers, where I developed a brain-based Resilience Model™ that we use to teach youth and adults the tools to cope with emotions, pain, and life's knocks. This model combines evidence-based practices from brain-based research, including tools from DBT, shame resilience research, self-compassion research, and mindfulness. Clients with eating disorders, anxiety, depression, general fear, school struggles, and work struggles are saying that it is changing their lives. This makes me happy, and I pledge to continue to grow and learn to deliver the latest interventions that are researched to be effective in giving clients a choice to cope with pain, fear, shame, anxiety, and other hard emotions by using tools instead of feeling their only choice is to numb.

This recovery thing is never ending.
Don't be frightened.
Upon the way, we will surely find ourselves.
We will.
Oh, yes, we will.
Then, our only job is to get out of our own way.

You've got this!
—*Robyn*

Resources

If you or your loved one is struggling with an eating disorder or other co-occurring illnesses, please know you are not alone.

Did you know that currently many major insurances pay for eating disorder treatment, and there are treatment facilities that also take Medicare or Medicaid?

Do you live in a rural area and don't have the professional support you need? Fear not, if you want recovery you can find the support you need.

Below is a list of helpful tools that can add additional support to your recovery.

- National Eating Disorders Association (NEDA): nationaleatingdisorders.org
- International Association of Eating Disorders Professionals Foundation (IAEDP): iaedp.site-ym.com (Under Membership/Members Directory)
- Eating Disorders Resource Catalogue: edcatalogue.com/organizations/
- Anxiety and Depression Association of America (ADAA): adaa.org/finding-help
- International OCD Foundation (IOCDF): iocdf.org/ocd-finding-help/find-help/
- Substance Abuse and Mental Health Services Administration (SAMHSA): samhsa.gov/find-treatment

About the Authors

Robyn Cruze, MA holds a master's degree in performing arts and is a sought-after keynote speaker, educating on the co-occurrence of substance and eating disorders, *The Body Conversation*—how to have a relationship with your body and the food you put in it, and all things mental health advocacy. She is the co-founder of a family mental health awareness initiative, Wide Wonder, which aims to make mental health and addiction recovery an everyday conversation. She also serves as the director of advocacy consultant at Eating Recovery Center. Robyn lives in Los Angeles, California.

Espra Andrus, LCSW is a clinical therapist who has specialized in working with individuals suffering with the full spectrum of eating disorders, mood disorders, and trauma for almost two decades. Espra is a Certified Daring Way™ Facilitator, living and teaching ways to live authentically instead of from shame. She is a co-founder of Life Launch Centers where she created the Resilience Model©, an 8-stage brain-based model with evidence-based tools for emotional and life resilience. Espra is passionate about living instead of numbing. She lives in St. George, Utah.